Fav©

MW00680491

for

FL - ESL Classes

by

Margaret S. Woodruff-Wieding, Ph.D.
and
Laura J. Ayala

ISBN 0-940296-70-5

Published by
Sky Oaks Productions, Inc.
P.O. Box 1102 • Los Gatos, CA 95031

Phone: (408) 395-7600
Fax: (408) 395-8440
e-mail: tprworld@aol.com

Free TPR Catalog upon Request

You can also order our TPR products from anywhere in the world by clicking on...

www.tpr-world.com

© Copyright, 1989, 2006

All Rights Reserved Worldwide. No part of this publication may be reproduced for any purpose, *including classroom instruction* by any individual or institution, *including schools,* nor may it be stored in a retrieval system, or transmitted in any form or by any means: electronic, magnetic tape, mechanical, photocopying, recording or otherwise, without permission in writing from an executive officer of **Sky Oaks Productions, Inc.**

This book is protected internationally by the Universal Copyright Convention of Geneva, Switzerland.

Table of Contents

Preface and Acknowledgments

Many of our activities and games are well known to language instructors. Most were used successfully in an experimental German program (that was honored with the Paul Pimsleur Award) at the University of Texas at Austin. The games have been fine-tuned since then as a result of our teaching experience.

Some games were developed by teaching assistants and faculty members working under the program director, Professor Janet K. Swaffar. Other games were inspired by descriptions in the articles and books listed in our bibliography, especially in *Learning Another Language Through Actions* by Dr. James J. Asher, the originator of TPR. Other resources include articles and books by Carton-Caprio, Dorry, Emmons, Grobe, Kohl, Lee, Schmidt, and Wagner, all of which are highly recommended to the reader. It was interesting to see that some teaching assistants invented games which we later found in established game anthologies. This should encourage all beginning language instructors to feel confident about making up their own games, since everyone with some feel for the playful nature of language learning will see certain game possibilities in their material.

The experimental project included not only college classes, but also a year-long curriculum prepared for first-year classes in four local high schools, and was supported by the National Endowment for the Humanities. Teachers in these four high schools and in some of the control-group high schools also designed and refined some games in this book.

We would like to thank all the instructors who allowed us to observe and take notes on the games and activities they developed. Special thanks to Janet Swaffar, whose idea this book was, to Rebecca Woodruff for her careful review of the manuscript, and to Del Wieding for his photographs and drawings.

Editor's Note: The writers welcome your comments and suggestions.

E-mail: wieding@onr.com *or* mwieding@tlu.edu

1. Introduction

Reading comprehension was the primary goal of the experimental program in which these games and activities were first used. The approach was based on five principles:

1. present language as **communication in context;**
2. teach **recognition before production;**
3. postpone **demands** for **error-free production** until a high level of comprehension is achieved;
4. present **grammar** as an **aspect of meaningful communication;**
5. use the **foreign language** in instruction as much as possible.

1. Present Language As Communication in Context

The core assumption of the program was that language learning should begin with **simple responses** that show understanding of what is heard or read and proceed with simple communication. Learning *about* a language is not the same as **experiencing language.** In effect, teachers were told to give people a bat and a ball and send them out into the game rather than to begin with illustrated lectures on how the bat hits the ball or with practice swings and pitches at imaginary balls.

The first hours of instruction started off by redefining the classroom as a place for **genuine communication** in the target language. This was achieved by applying James J. Asher's **TPR** (Total Physical Response) learning strategy of making **physical responses** to **oral commands:** partly because such procedures dramatically emphasize communication, but even more because this strategy is consistent with the principle that **production naturally follows comprehension.**

Pre-Reading Phase

The first four weeks of the program consisted primarily of spoken instructions to which students responded with physical actions. Speaking was not required, but after the second week, with encouragement from the instructor, most students chose to give the teacher and other students instructions like those they had been given. For example, teachers had demonstrated simple commands such as "**stand up**" and "**point to**" while describing their actions. Students were then given commands and responded in groups or individually. After each set of new commands had been practiced, students indicated by saying "**yes**" or "**no**" whether or not instructors were doing what they were saying. As the students' attention span expanded, they were able easily to perform several commands in sequence, for example, "point to the light, then stand up, breathe deeply, and sit down."

Both teacher and students were encouraged to **play with the language**, experimenting with novel and even bizarre combinations, since experiences out of the ordinary aid foreign language learners in vocabulary retention. The vocabulary was printed in the student syllabus, along with occasional assignments for written commands creatively recombining certain verbs and nouns. (For a step-by-step guide in how this is done, see Asher, 1986, Garcia, 1988, and Woodruff, 1986.)

Beginning to Read

In the **fifth week**, students began to read short illustrated texts for the main idea. They were told: "Just as you have relied on actions to demonstrate meaning, you will now infer the meaning of phrases from pictures, context in the readings, similarity to English and German words you already know, and rephrasing by the teacher in German words you already know.

Practicing **educated guessing** is of more value to you than memorizing lists of German-English equivalents, and will help you learn to read German more rapidly and efficiently than you can by relying on a dictionary. The reading skills that you practice, such as previewing a story, predicting what you will learn from it, and inferring meanings, may even help you to read English more efficiently. The more you read, the better you will read, so we ask you to read a chapter a day as homework and sometimes to sightread one- to two-page stories in class, reading for the main idea and for answers to questions rather than translating."

Care was taken to keep the classroom a creative and active place. Students continued to give and respond to instructions using the vocabulary of the readings and began pantomiming the action of the stories. They often drew pictures to demonstrate their comprehension.

Writing and Speaking

Writing and speaking accompanied the listening and reading practice, but **students were not expected to produce error-free sentences** at the same level of complexity that they understood when they read and listened to German. Such demands would have led to failure for many students, and it was important to give them **a successful experience** in using the language.

Vocabulary Learning

Creating a context for foreign-language communication helps solve a problem all foreign-language teachers face: how to help students learn vocabulary efficiently. Learning words from lively classroom presentations involving pictures and actions and stories is not perceived as drudgery, as is often the case with list memorization. Moreover, memorization is more efficient if the items to be learned are **linked in a meaningful sequence,** rather than isolated or simply paired with their English equivalents.

Review and variation of structures and vocabulary already learned also took place within a **context of communication.** Talking about props, pictures, and parts of the room, even guessing games as to where an object had been hidden, were sometimes spontaneous but were often carefully planned as **reentry of certain structures** (question, command, statement) and certain vocabulary.

Spontaneously created **novel situations** were often the best for fixing words in students' memories. In one of the second-semester classes, a student told the class dramatically in German that an object had fallen from a **scaffold** in a construction project that she passed on her way to class; she used the word for scaffold because it had appeared in the story assigned for that day. Though the word was not mentioned again for several weeks, the entire class showed that they recalled its meaning when it appeared in a later story, apparently because what happened earlier had focused their attention on the word in a naturally memorable way.

2. Teach Recognition before Production

Recognition or **comprehension** seems to be a natural first stage before production of language. Taking this into account seems eventually to lead to more efficient recall and production, when the students are ready. Although students were certainly active while learning in our program, **physically demonstrating comprehension** of what they heard and read, they were practicing receptive more than productive language skills.

When they spoke, moreover, they were not producing German of the same complexity or at the same rate at which they were learning it. Some researchers (Asher, 1986) feel that interference occurs when speaking (whether repetition or recall) and comprehension (or acquisition) are attempted simultaneously. In other words, practice is not necessarily the same as acquisition. Delaying demands for speaking until some comprehension is achieved may prevent this interference and increase retention as well as prevent frustration.

Only after a few weeks of listening to German and **showing their understanding through physical actions** were students expected to produce their own sentences. At the beginning of the semester they had been told that they would have a chance to utter directions in German to manipulate the behavior of the teachers. Even before the teachers began suggesting it, around the end of the second week, many students began **speaking spontaneously,** giving humorous commands that were recombinations of words and phrases the teacher had used.

Throughout the first year of German the same basic procedure continued: exposure to a set of structures and vocabulary through reading or listening; showing recognition of their meaning and the situations in which they were appropriate; and recalling them in an appropriate context.

3. Postpone Demands for Error-Free Production

Effectiveness of communication was the main criterion for judging production in the first year. "Global" errors were corrected, because such errors actually interfered with communication. Usually "local" errors, those that did not interfere with communication, were ignored; at most, the teacher **casually** repeated the statement correctly.

When a student said something that would not make sense to a native speaker, the teacher stopped, found out what the student was trying to say, and helped the individual say it correctly. Much more class time was spent in **eliciting responses** and reinforcing them than in correcting sentences with global errors, for students rarely produced such errors.

Eliciting responses is a better use of class time in the first year, when students are just beginning to learn that a foreign language can be used for interesting communication. Demanding correctness in all sentences produced in the first year is at best premature. The student's desire to achieve accuracy can be one of the language teacher's greatest aids, but it usually depends on the student's having time to develop an interest in the foreign language and culture.

4. Present Grammar in Meaningful Contexts

Since the students needed to see language as communication in a personally meaningful context, they were rarely asked to transform isolated sentences. The goal was to make all sentences used in class-work or tests part of a discussion, description, dialogue, or story. Moreover, since the **major objective** for the **first year** was **comprehension**, grammar was presented as an aid to understanding: students were taught what they needed in order to understand the text. They were taught, for example, to use the German preference for capitalizing the initial letter of nouns as a cue to help them in their "educated guessing" of word meanings by narrowing down the range of possibilities.

As mentioned earlier, teaching first-semester students *about* grammar was felt to be rather like teaching someone to play baseball by conducting a seminar on the theory of contacting the ball with the bat. Theory is interesting, but **discussing it in detail is more appropriate for advanced students.**

One takes beginners out on the field and gives them the ball and bat. This was done literally as well as figuratively, since balls were used as objects of description in the classroom. As they threw foam rubber balls around the classroom and talked casually with the teacher about what they were doing, some students hardly suspected that they were transforming statements to questions, dependent clauses to independent ones, present to past tense as directed in a game that was really rather like a disguised standard structure drill.

5. Use the Foreign Language As Much As Possible

Students learn more when common **classroom interactions** take place in the foreign language. One of the benefits of starting a first-year program with **commands** and **games** that direct the behavior of the students is that the students then comprehend a basic repertoire of instructions for classroom activities that can be used throughout their years of study such as "Go to the board and write on it" or "Put your chairs in a small circle."

Beginning with commands makes it possible for the instructor to speak the target language through the class hour from the first meeting of the class. Of course, there will normally be some need for communication in the native language; however, even tests and student syllabi, sometimes so detailed that they seemed more like lesson plans, were almost **entirely in German**. Thus, students were given the vocabulary they needed for realistic, non-simulated communication with the teacher about daily activities.

At the beginning of the first semester, students were told: "Because discussion in English interrupts your language learning, you are encouraged to ask any questions you may have about German grammar at the **end of the hour**. Translation of phrases and sentences into English will be avoided in favor of translation into actions or pictures. You will remember words and phrases better if you have visualized their meaning or acted them out. Whenever possible, we will demonstrate meaning with actions, pictures, flash cards, or explanations in German. However, you may be asked occasionally for the English meaning of isolated words to verify comprehension."

When teachers use the foreign language for classroom instructions and announcements and informal friendly greetings, such communication begins to feel natural and obvious to students. If, in addition, a **relaxed** and **happy classroom atmosphere** prevails, many students will communicate in the language voluntarily.

The instructors of the experimental program in which these games and activities were developed felt that extensive aural **comprehension** practice and **playful** use of the foreign language seemed to foster reading comprehension skills superior to those attained in programs with more stress on production grammar and fewer challenges to students' imagination and ability at inference.

Additional factors that may have been crucial for the success of the reading program were systematic development of reading skills and designing homework assignments and test questions to capture student interest through novelty and personal meaningfulness.

A modified version of the detailed syllabus used in the first four weeks of our program may be found in Woodruff (1986).

2. Getting Started with Games

These structured activities for **playful** foreign language communication are intended to stimulate teachers' imaginations to design exercises that suit their classroom needs.

GETTING STUDENTS INVOLVED

Language production is essentially creative, involving variations of basic patterns. We demonstrate this to our students by practicing with carefully designed games that involve not only **recycling of vocabulary and structures** but also **playfulness.** If the teacher presents language practice in a playful manner and treats it as a low-key challenge like a game, students will perceive practice as pleasant and interesting, and their motivation to participate will increase.

Stressing communication (first comprehension and later production) keeps students alert and prevents resistance to learning. We want to **build up students' confidence** by showing that they can use what they are learning for genuine communication.

The term "game" is used loosely to include **simulations** and **game-like learning activities.** Even better, we can present the entire process of learning to understand and speak a foreign language as an interesting challenge rather like a game.

It is helpful to point out to students that learning by *using* a language is a natural approach. Its effectiveness is suggested by the fact that children learn their native languages through play and communicative interaction, as Asher (1986) has pointed out in numerous articles.

Of course, games also help when students have trouble concentrating on more routine parts of the lesson. Playing almost any game in the foreign language is better than persisting with an activity to which students cannot pay attention. Games tend to **improve** both **group dynamics** and **student involvement.** Photocopying games and descriptions and stapling them onto 3x5 or 4x6 cards that can always be found in the instructor's briefcase or on a desk is a convenient way to ensure that the games will be used regularly.

The games that work well in a given classroom should be used over and over, since this gives students a sense of security and continuity; however, they should be **repeated** with **new content.**

CRITERIA FOR SELECTING OR INVENTING GAMES

The games should be played in the foreign language. However, the ground rules can be explained in the native language, if necessary.

We should use games with **rules** that are so **simple** that little class time is taken up in introducing them. For beginners, vocabulary used in games should be primarily **familiar vocabulary** or vocabulary targeted for teaching in the same semester.

We should use only those games that are related either to the culture of the foreign country or to practicing comprehension or production of the language in context. For example, a competition between teams of students to list as many German words as possible that begin with a certain letter of the alphabet is not related to German culture or to any meaningful aspect of the structure of the language.

Organizing by alphabet is abstract and does not offer enough context to make the activity seem related to any real-life application. Moreover, it is primarily a recall test rather than a learning game.

Even tests can be learning activities rather than exercises in recall if, for example, teachers write **short anecdotes** with **familiar vocabulary** and ask students to either listen to or read the anecdote and list all the foods Juan bought at the market or all the sports played by the teenagers in Frankfurt. In such a test, students learn to listen or read more efficiently; they learn cultural details; and they may learn new vocabulary that they infer from the context.

The **games** in our book are organized into **three sections**. The first section centers around **learning categories** such as alphabet, numbers, sentence negation, or giving commands. In the next section, games are **organized by technique**. These include such categories as guessing, simulations, and physical response activities. In the third section, all games are classified by the **type** of material required, such as pictures or cards.

The simpler and easier games appear at the beginning of each subsection. However, almost all of our games can be used at beginning, intermediate, and advanced levels, by choosing the vocabulary and syntax appropriate for the level.

3. Games by Learning Category

ALPHABET AND SPELLING

Introduction: Recite alphabet aloud in unison, grouping letters in small rhythmical groups, using an alphabet song if possible. Have each student say one letter, going around in a circle.

Recognition stage: Students answer "yes" or "no" as the teacher points to letters on the board and asks questions such as: "Is this a *q*?"

> *Variation:* Students at the board each write a letter of the alphabet dictated by the teacher. Students then step away from the board to reveal a word or sentence for the class to read aloud. We have found that students appreciate the use of humor or personal words (e.g., the name of their school mascot).

> *Variation:* Spell students' names and have them stand up when they recognize their own names.

> *Benefit:* **The physical activity** helps keep them alert.

Production stage: One to three students are sent out of the room. The class agrees on a sentence and writes it on the board, leaving blanks in place of some letters. Student(s) return to guess the missing letters. With encouragement, students will choose sentences with personal or humorous content.

Gregorio is filling in the blanks to complete the sentence "Tomorrow is our first exam." He asks other students questions such as "Does an *m* go here?"

Personalized practice: Have students spell their first, middle, and last names for other students to write on the board.

> *Variation:* For additional fun, student at board can be asked to guess whether the full name the student dictated was in fact the student's real name or a fictitious one. Many students enjoy choosing a foreign-language name, whether for one day or an entire semester or year.

Game: Bingo, with one student as caller and the rest playing. Use letters of a foreign-language word at top of columns instead of B-I-N-G-O, especially words with letter combinations that commonly cause spelling problems, such as French E-A-U in B-E-A-U-X or German I-E in S-P-I-E-L. Students are ready to play Bingo for as long as the teacher will allow. (Also try Ramiro Garcia's **TPR Bingo** [Garcia 1988b].)

Recycling with other topics: Two or three students go to the board and write alphabet letters at the teacher's dictation to form a word. The teacher's instructions are not in order, but rather by position ("write *e* left of *n*"). Thus students practice position words as well as letters.

When the word is formed, students read it aloud. The words dictated should correspond to material currently being taught and be related to each other: either the same content category, such as food, or the same word family (**typewriter, typist, typical,** etc.). We have found that students enjoy the mental challenge that comes from focusing on two factors, **position** and **alphabet letter**, at the same time.

> *Variation:* The teacher can use alphabet review as a point of departure for a related topic of conversation. Example: "Write *e, b* left of *e, d* right of *e*. Read the word. Where do we find a bed? When do we go to bed, at night or in the morning?"

> *Benefits:* Frequent **recycling** of previously taught material along with new material gives students the intermittent, repeated **re-exposure** to earlier material that they need for **long-term retention**.

CHANGING CASE

This activity works well with changes from nominative case (subject) to accusative (direct object). For example, in German a special ending is added to the article before the noun for masculine accusative, but not for feminine, neuter, or plural. Name something, such as a pencil: "Ein Bleistift." Then tell the students you're taking a pencil, and do so: "Ich nehme einen Bleistift." Repeat this with other props, including at the end feminine and neuter nouns as well.

Then give each student an object or picture and have them stand or sit in a circle so that they can see each other's objects. Take an object yourself and model for them: "That's a _____. I'm eating/drinking a _____." (Pantomime it.) Or: "I see a _____."

Now, substituting the name of the noun he holds, each student in turn says the pair of sentences modeled by the teacher. Then each student in turn points at an object held by any of the other students and says, "I want a _____," upon which that student must bring it to her. Asking for something from another student or from the teacher brings a smile to the face of even the most solemn student. The reason is apparently that the shift in focus from the speaker's structural or grammatical accuracy to meaningful interaction with others makes students feel less inhibited. Students frequently feel relaxed enough to make absurd, humorous, or very personal requests in this context: "I want an elephant; three bottles of wine; a castle in Spain."

> _Variation:_ Student says, "Bring me a ____, please."

CHANGING TENSE

The teacher gives commands, then asks not only what a person is doing but also what she will do (before she does it) and what she did (after she does it). It is helpful to begin by reviewing verb transformations with a series of examples. "Bob, go to the door." Before Bob gets up: "Bob will go to the door." While Bob goes to the door: "Bob is going to the door." After Bob arrives: "Bob went to the door."

Students are divided into teams. If students answer with the correct tenses, their team wins points.

Another sample series using a different verb may be necessary before the game begins. **Timing** is crucial in the success of this game, if students are to understand the connections between the actions and the utterances. If timing is off, so that the wrong tense is used (e.g., the present tense is used for an activity that is already completed), students feel either confused or irritated, depending on how well they understand the tense discrimination.

CHANGING VOICE

To practice transforming a statement in the active voice to one in the passive voice: First the teacher, then students place an object somewhere and say, "I'm putting the _____ on the _____." A fellow student is cued to say, "The _____ is being put/ was put/ will be put on the _____" (practicing **only one tense and person at a time** until all forms are familiar).

DESCRIBING ACTIONS

Throw a foam rubber ball to a student and ask:
  What am I doing? *(You're throwing a ball.)*
  What are you doing? *(I'm catching a ball.)*
  What is he doing? *(He's catching a ball.)*
  Where is the ball? *(In John's hand.)*
  Who has it? *(John has the ball.)*
  What are you saying? *(I'm saying he has the ball.)*
  Tell him to throw the ball. *(Throw the ball.)*
  What is she telling him? *(She's telling him to throw the ball.)*
  Use a modal auxiliary! *(She's telling him he must throw the ball.)*
Throw me the ball. What did I do? *(You caught the ball.)*
  What shall I do with the ball now? (Invite absurd and humorous responses, for example: *Put the ball on Bill's head.)*

This game was invented by one of the older, more conservative college professors in our program. He enjoyed it tremen-dously, and so did his students.

> **Variation:** Practice the correct use of *he* and *she, him* and *her:* Who is catching the ball, he or she? Are you throwing the ball to him or to her?

> **Variation:** Use other paired verbs like *give/take, drop/pick up,* or *spill/clean up:* Is Ann taking or giving the hat? Am I picking up the box or dropping it?

Benefits: Although this is a drill, genuine communication is taking place; also, the students pay attention and participate through actions that reinforce their words.

DESCRIBING OBJECTS

The **speaker** says, **"I see something you don't see, and it is red."** Students then **ask questions** to help determine which object is meant, or the speaker gives additional clues. The name of the correct item must be **familiar vocabulary.**

The speaker should be warned not to give away the object by looking at it while it is being guessed. Students generally relax and smile during this game. It allows some students with good memories who are anxious about speaking to **experience success** by demonstrating their comprehension.

> ***Benefit:*** Besides helping students **use new descriptive adjectives,** this activity practices general vocabulary and grammar structures, such as question formation. It can be used at beginning levels with descriptive terms such as *large, short,* or *blue,* at intermediate levels with words like *round, soft,* or *heavy,* and at the higher levels with words such as *wrinkled, bumpy,* or *stiff.*

GETTING ACQUAINTED

Activities for beginning classes that lead to simple, personal exchanges between students and teacher can take place from the first week of class on and can vary in topic and structural complexity as the year progresses. The activities are designed to be short and to be used over and over as warm-ups or wind-downs in class.

Exchanging names: Students sit in a circle. The teacher says, "My name is _____" and asks students what their names are; they may answer with name only at first. Then the teacher looks each student in turn in the eye and says his name.

When you don't remember a student's name, ask again. Then ask a student to recite the names in order, with eye contact, just as you have done. Other students should supply names if a student pauses for a long time. We have found that some students have remarkable memories (or large circles of acquaintances) and enjoy showing the instructor how much better they can perform the task.

Note: By the second week of class, students should all answer, "My name is ___."

Greetings and small talk: For roll call, exchange greetings and ask one personal question of each student, such as, "How old are you?" Students may answer in complete sentences if they wish or give short answers.

Likes and dislikes: Ask a student about a **personal preference**. The student answers and asks the next student the same question, for example, "What do you like to eat?"

This game takes considerable time in a large class; it is better to shift to a variation after the question has been asked 8 or 10 times to prevent student boredom. However, if your students are ready for a **fast pace**, it is possible to give everyone the chance to express a preference occasionally so that no one feels left out.

> ***Variation:*** Variations in questions about *likes* and *dislikes* are endless. Another day you might use the question, "Where do you like to go?" and afterwards you and students might try to repeat where each student likes most to go.
>
> For example, "Bob likes to go fishing, Jane likes to go to the beach, and I like to go to the movies." A long chain of phrases is challenging, but we found that most students can remember it by association with their fellow students' names and faces.

Self-assessments: Students describe themselves individually with two or three adjectives chosen from a list on the board ("I'm small and nervous but happy") and asks the next student, "And what sort of person are you?"

> ***Variation:*** Before students individually describe themselves, they describe a few of the students who have already had a turn: "He's small and nervous but happy, she's enthusiastic and friendly, and I'm loyal and hardworking."

Benefits: Students **practice concentration** and **chaining phrases** together with connecting words; they **internalize** words other than just those they chose to describe themselves.

To prevent students from choosing safe and boring words, put interesting words on the board and restrict them to your list. More authentic communication may result. Examples: ambitious, brave, candid, cautious, curious, cynical, funny, generous, impatient, impractical, lazy, modest, old-fashioned, punctual, reckless, silly, sophisticated, vain, versatile, wise.

Personal interviews: Interviewer asks the interviewee personal questions on a given topic:
   Do you have a brother (sister, cousin)? _(Pause for the answer.)_
   What is his (her) name? _(Pause for the answer.)_
   What do you like to do together? _(Pause for the answer.)_
When the interview is complete, the interviewer then restates the set of answers to the group, in the form of a short description of the person.

The interview itself can be done in pairs by everyone at once or with the group listening. Students are more likely to produce an interesting description if you carefully develop some **interesting** and **unusual questions** using familiar vocabulary. Descriptions are more likely to be coherent if you provide a **written model** with **blanks** for students to fill in, allowing them to focus on content and speaking practice.

Sample questions: Do you like to use computers? To play video games? How often do you go to the movies? Would you rather rent videos for a VCR? What do you eat for a snack after school? At what time of day do you watch TV? What kind of part-time job would you like?

Sample written model: _____ has (no brothers), (and/but) (she/he) has (one sister). (Her) name is _____. They like to shop for _____, play _____, listen to _____, and go out to eat _____.

GIVING COMMANDS

Perform an action and then describe it: "I'm going to the board." Give the students, in groups and afterwards individually, corresponding commands: "Go to the board!" Say, "Now tell me!" and they tell you to go to the board. Manipulating the behavior of the teacher and other students was our students' favorite game.

Variation: For languages with more than one word for "you," the teacher can explain the social distinctions between the forms. In German, for example, students can be asked to use the **familiar form** for giving commands to other students and the **polite form** for the teacher.

Variation: After students have practiced giving commands and acquired some vocabulary, hold up an object and invite them to formulate a command by asking:

What should I do with the _____?

What should Mary do with the _____?

What should Mary and John do with the _____?

Instead of supplying the object to be used in the command, say, "Give Mary a command with 'run'," and the student might say, "Run to the chalkboard."

Benefits: We found that students enjoyed giving commands more when the action or object was specified in this way, so that they were not under so much pressure to be clever. This variation also prevented them from trying to think in their native language of a clever command for which they had no vocabulary. Occasionally, and especially after giving commands is a familiar and comfortable activity, students need to be entirely free to choose from the vocabulary they already know.

Variation: To teach students to remember **longer chains of words or phrases** it is best to review **familiar commands** in combination. For example, "Pick up a pencil slowly, put it quickly behind your ear, and then put your hand on the desk."

Ask the students to wait until a command is finished before they begin responding. Students love the challenge involved in this task and the humorous nature of some of the combinations. A syntactically complex or simply long sentence (such as the one in the preceding paragraph) is quite manageable for them when their task is a physical response that demonstrates comprehension.

Relaxation: The teacher or student gives directions in the form of **commands** for **simple calisthenics**, demonstrating each step before directing the group to perform it. Nonsensical combination commands involving physical activity also help: "Run to the wastebasket and put your notebook in it, then sit down on the floor next to the wastebasket."

> *Benefits:* These exercises help vary class routine but also help students relax from the stress or tension of trying to understand and speak a foreign language.

HEARING AND PRONOUNCING

Say two words that differ by one vowel or consonant, and ask students whether they are alike or different. Then say the *same* word twice, and ask, "Alike or different?"

Write two words on the board that differ by one vowel or consonant, and label them #1 and #2. Say one word and ask, "Number 1 or number 2?"

Students identify whether the two words are **alike** or **different**, or whether the vowels are **short** or **long**; then which word from the board is being said, #1 or #2. Each correct answer wins points for a team.

Example: Say "Listen: /i/, /e/. Now listen: pin, pen: alike or different? Pen, pen: alike or different?" Repeat with similar examples until answer given is usually correct.

Now write on board:

#1	#2
pin	pen
bin	Ben

Say "Am I saying #1 or #2? Ben." Repeat with similar examples until answer given is usually correct.

Pictures of objects with **similar names** can be shown and students can be asked whether teachers are pointing at the **hut** or the **hat**, the **rope** or the **robe**; whether teachers are naming **Picture 1** or **Picture 2**. Students can also respond to sentences by showing or holding out props, e.g., "I'd like to look at your back/book"; "May I borrow your pin/pen?"

Follow-up activities: Students say the word to which the teacher points on the board. They write the words from dictation. They copy the appropriate contrasted word into blanks in sentences. They make up sentences with the words.

> ***Variation:*** Where intonation or stress marks the difference between statement and question, or question and command, ask students to raise their hands if they hear a question and keep them down if they hear a command (or statement).

> ***Variation:*** Students identify whether a word is spoken with foreign-language pronunciation or with American pronunciation. You ask, "French or American?" This is most helpful with words that are spelled the same or nearly the same in the native language and the second language. We have found that these are the words which are most likely to be mispronounced.

> ***Benefits:*** Students pronounce better if they have first learned to distinguish among different sounds or stresses and intonations.

MAKING STATEMENTS AND ASKING QUESTIONS

Description of actions in first, second, and third person, singular and plural, should be practiced: **one new ending at a time, using familiar vocabulary.**

The teacher performs an action and describes what is happening: "What am I doing? I'm giving Sally a book." Then the teacher asks a student to do the same thing: "Give Sally a book!" and asks, "What are you doing?"

It may be necessary to model the pattern ("I'm _____ing _____.") several times or even write it on the board. Giving commands and asking students what they are doing as they respond is a good way to ensure that specific words are reviewed, but the teacher can also say, "Do something!" and then ask, "What are you doing?"

It should be made clear to the students that when they choose actions to perform they will need to do something that they already have the vocabulary to describe, whether it is something simple that the teacher has often instructed them to do in earlier classes ("Go to the board!") or a novel and humorous variation combining old vocabulary, such as walking slowly to the table and sitting down quickly under it.

Later, students can practice description, in second or third person, of actions performed by the teacher and other students. They may pattern their responses after the teacher's cues, which give them the vocabulary they need. For example:

Teacher: "Give Sally a book. He's giving Sally a book. Is he giving Sally a book?"

Student: "Yes, he's giving Sally a book."

After three or four identical exchanges with different students, the teacher asks: "What is he doing?" and cues a student with "He...." After a week or so of practice of the basic game with regular verbs, there is no need to avoid irregular verbs that have been introduced. As soon as students are comfortable with the pattern, they can divide into teams. The teams win a point if a team member describes an action correctly when it is their turn.

> *Variation:* With high-frequency verbs whose stems change from one person to another (such as "to be" in some languages), a circle drill involving the entire class works well. Students can answer the classmate to their left and ask the classmate to their right in the following pattern, as everyone listens: "I'm sixteen years old. How old are you?"

> *Variation:* Give a student a command, for example to touch his nose, and during the action, say, "You're touching your nose." Tell the student to ask another student quickly while still doing it, "What am I doing?"

> Gesture to the other student to answer by describing the action as you did: "You're touching your nose." Have several students answer the student's question as to what he is doing. When students are familiar with this routine, they can continue the game without teacher intervention.

The first student asks another student to continue the chain by giving someone a command: "Javier, give Jane a command." Jane then asks various students as she carries out Javier's command, "What am I doing?"

NEGATING SENTENCES

Tell the students that the class will be playing a game called "**Argue with me.**" When you point at something and say it is something it isn't, they should argue with you by saying, "**No, it isn't.**" If your statement is true, they should agree, "**Yes, it is.**" For example, say, "The chalkboard is pink."

Or make statements about the weather, who's in class, etc., mixing accurate ones with inaccurate ones. Similarly, perform an action such as hopping and say, "I'm hopping," or "Am I hopping?" They say, "**Yes, you are.**" or "**No, you aren't.**"

> _**Benefits:**_ We found that student motivation is highest when they are encouraged to correct the instructor or argue with the instructor in structured, legitimate situations like this. Later in the semester, students felt comfortable politely pointing out an accidental error to the instructor. This appeared to increase their feeling of responsibility for their own learning.

> _**Variation:**_ Ask the students to say the complete sentences, such as "Yes, that's a _____"; "No, you're not _____ing." After students have mastered positive to negative transformation, try negative to positive (remind them that this is still arguing with you). For example, say, "This room doesn't have four walls." A student replies, "Yes, it does."

> _**Variation:**_ Students alternate making statements and negating what the last student said:
> He likes sausage; he doesn't like sausage.
> The room is hot; the room isn't hot.
> Bob has a new jacket; Bob doesn't have a new jacket.
> Mary has some money; Mary doesn't have any money.

NUMBERS AND COUNTING

Initial lesson: Point to numbers written in sequence on the board from 1 to 20, and pronounce them for the students. Point to numbers in sequence and ask the students to repeat after you.

Recognition activities: Students listen to the numbers and demonstrate their understanding *without* saying the numbers.

1. Say four or five numbers in various combinations, while students just listen, and then ask questions about the combinations.

   Examples: 5-7-9-11-13. Even or odd?
                   20-19-18-17-16. Forward or backward?

2. Have two students write the numbers 1-20 on the board (each writing ten). Call some of the numbers at random; the students take turns crossing them out as they are called.

   Note: This activity also works well as a review of numbers from 1-100. To <u>recycle numbers</u> use other topics, such as telling time, weights and measures, dates, sums of money, and telephone numbers.

Recognition and sound imitation: Students still focus primarily on the meaning of the numbers they hear, but their responses require them to repeat a number they have heard.

- Point to a numeral (e.g., 3) on the board and ask a student *or*-questions, such as, "Is it thirteen or three?" *Answer:* "Three."

   Benefit: This is particularly helpful in contrasting numbers that are easily confused with each other, such as German *dreizehn* and *dreißig* (13 and 30).

- Teacher says, without pointing to a number, "I'm thinking of a number. It's higher than fourteen. Is it twelve or fifteen?" *Answer:* "Fifteen."

   Benefits: As students continue to focus on meaning, they imitate the numbers pronounced by the teacher, thus lessening the need for number repetition drills.

Production: Students recall the numbers they have learned as a result of previous recognition activities.

- Students go around the room in order, each saying a number in sequence.
- A student claps or knocks on the table, asks "how often," and points at another student, who answers "three times."
- Students count aloud in unison or individually: by 2's (even or odd), 3's, 4's, 5's, 10's, backwards.

> *Variation:* Counting can be cued by a large, soft ball which is thrown from one student to another. Students at all levels enjoy the surprise of being called on by having a ball thrown. They laugh when the ball is missed, and are willing to practice counting, for example, by 500's to 100,000 backwards as well as forwards.
> *Example:* 100,000; 99,500; 99,000; 98,500...
>
> *Benefit:* Counting large numbers is particularly helpful for languages such as Spanish, in which prices must often be calculated in thousands.

- Bring a stopwatch and have students compete to count from 1 to 60 in 60 seconds. The closest wins.

- Class stands and students count by 1's, saying an animal sound such as *cockadoodledoo* in the foreign language whenever they come to a number with 7 or a multiple of 7 in it. Anyone who says the number instead of the animal sound is "out" and sits down. Repeat the activity with a different animal sound and a different key number.

> *Benefit:* An entertaining way for students to learn that animal sounds are often represented differently in different languages. This is just as popular with older adults as with junior high, high school, and college students.

- Students are given different amounts of real or play money; they count it and report how much they have altogether and how much of each coin and bill.

- Students roll dice, call out the numbers separately, then add them and say their sum.

Note: This activity works well with students divided into several small groups.

• Do math problems; later do problems involving real, culturally accurate situations which use numbers (liters used per 100 kilometers, shopping prices, etc.). Oral and written.

Games: Students practice the numbers they have learned in competitive activities such as these:

• Bingo, with one student as caller and others playing.

> *Variation:* Bingo with addition. Instead of "11" say "6 + 5."

• In two teams, students compete to guess how many pennies someone has, how tall someone is, how long it takes someone to walk to his home from the school or college. If possible, use the foreign currency and system of measurement. The one who guesses closest wins a point for her team.

> *Variation:* This can be done with students in groups of three. They each write down the information above on a sheet of paper that they conceal from the other two students. Taking turns, each student asks the remaining two to guess a fact. The closest guesser receives a point, and the student with the most points at the end wins.

> *Benefits:* By working in small groups, students get more speaking practice. If motivation is needed to keep them on task, the teacher might offer each winner a token reward, such as points they can earn toward dropping the lowest quiz or homework grade.

Recycling: Student syllabi often are not built around topics involving numbers at the time when numbers are presented. A natural recycling of numbers can occur when such topics do come up.

Address and phone number. Students ask and write down each other's addresses and phone numbers (in the format used in the foreign culture).

Benefit: In college classes it is helpful to use this activity early so that students who miss class will have someone to call for the assignment.

Dates and holidays. Ask questions about today's date, tomorrow's date, yesterday's date, the dates of approaching holidays, and birthdays.

Variation: Students write their birthdays (day and month) and their names on cards. The teacher reads the birthdays but not the names aloud; the students listen for their own birthdays and say, "That is my birthday. My birthday is the __th of _____." Then the teacher reads through all cards again and students write each class-mate's name and birthday from dictation in order to make a birthday book.

Shopping. Students inquire about prices and make change in simulated shopping activities. They ask, "How much is that?" They give the "salesperson" $5.00 for an item that costs $4.60, and the salesperson counts out the change: "Seventy, eighty, ninety, five dollars."

Travel. Students solve schedule problems using a real or simplified train timetable from a country where the foreign language is spoken. We have found that students from towns where public transportation is rarely used need a careful introduction to reading bus or train timetables before they can proceed with the main activity. This activity is generally appropriate after the first sixty hours of instruction.

PARTS OF THE BODY AND GROOMING

Spread out over a three- to ten-day period, each of these activities should be **performed in sequence.**

1. Tell a simple story about getting up in the morning and getting ready for school, acting it out as you go along. Use parts of the body, nouns such as *comb* and *brush,* and "grooming" verbs.

2. Retell the story with all students carrying out the pantomime at their seats.

3. Ask one student to recreate the story, using actions alone; you describe her actions.

4. Ask another student to recreate the story, using actions alone, while the class takes turn describing his actions (beginning students may use incomplete sentences or verb phrases such as "washing" at this point).

5. Distribute a printed version of the story and have a student read it aloud for the entire group to act out at their seats.

6. Have one student pantomime the story by memory while the class takes turn describing her actions, using sentences from the printed story.

7. Give students commands to perform all the actions.

8. Have students give commands to direct you or a student through the entire sequence of actions in the story.

You will want to devote only part of each class period to these sequence activities so that students review and reinforce their learning without having a chance to become bored with the topic. Here is a sample story:

It's 6:30 a.m. The alarm clock is ringing. A student wakes up, blinks her eyes, and yawns. Then she stands up and stretches her arms toward the ceiling. She laughs and shakes her head. She goes to the mirror and looks deep into her eyes. They are red from all the studying she did last night. She takes a shower and dries herself off. She dries her ears, her face, her arms, then her legs, and finally her feet. She takes her toothbrush and brushes her teeth. She brushes her hair with a hairbrush. She cleans her shoes. Now she's ready. Oh, no! Where are her clothes?

PLURALS AND TELLING HOW MANY

Students use the **plural forms** of familiar nouns. Gather several items together in sets of at least two. Hold two or more of a given item (e.g., pen) up to a student and say, "Touch one (pen) if I say it in the singular and two or more if I say it in the plural."

Then have students complete the sentences "That's a _____." when you touch one object and "Those are _____." when you touch two of them. They can make their own sentences, touching first one and then more objects and saying first, "This is a _____," followed by "These are _____." This is especially useful for languages such as German with many different ways of forming plurals.

POSSESSIVE ADJECTIVES AND BELONGING

Review possessive adjectives by pointing and saying:
This shirt belongs to **me**. It's **my** shirt.
This shirt *(pointing)* belongs to **him**. It's **his** shirt.
This shirt *(pointing)* belongs to **her**. It's **her** shirt.
This shirt *(pointing)* belongs to **you**. It's **your** shirt.

Then ask a student, "Show me my shirt" (and the student demonstrates understanding by **pointing** to your shirt). Then proceed with:
Show me **your** shirt.
Show me **his** shirt.
Show me **her** shirt.

Then have students say, about any object they can name in the room: "This (shirt) belongs to (name of student). It's **(his/her)** (shirt)." Students enjoy seeing the instructor jokingly claim ownership of students' possessions.

> *Variation:* Positive, comparative, and superlative forms of such adjectives as "large" and "small" can be practiced in a similar fashion: "This book is **small**. Jim's book is **smaller**. Bill's book is the **smallest**."
>
> Then, "Show me a **small** book; a **smaller** book; the **smallest** book." Then students can take turns walking around the room and comparing sets of two or three objects: "This book is **thin**. This book is **thinner**. This book is the **thinnest**."
>
> Other adjectives that may be used in many classrooms: large, thick, new, old, tall, short, light (color), dark (color), bright (color), dirty, clean, hot, cold.

RECOGNIZING RELATED WORDS

Give **beginning students** words in the foreign language that most of them would already know, such as *hors d'oeuvres* or *Kinder-*

garten, and have them supply the native-language definitions. Or give them a list of foreign-language words related to native-language words, such as *schreiben-scribe,* and have them guess the equivalents. Since cognate relationships are hard for many students to see, it can be helpful to offer students a chart of systematic correspondences, as between German *t* and English *d: tanzen = dance.* This can be used as a team competition, with points for correct answers.

> **_Benefits:_** In seeing how much they already know, students gain confidence in their ability to learn the foreign language.

TELLING TIME

Initial lesson: Give each student materials for making a paper-plate clock (paper plate, colored construction paper, metal brads, scissors). Have them set times you name on the individual clocks they have made and hold them up to show you. We found that college students enjoyed this activity, which allows the instructor to verify comprehension quickly.

When the instructor called out *Zweiundzwanzig Uhr fünfzehn* (22.15, or 10:15 p.m.), Kyle set the paper clock for 10:15 and showed his clock to the rest of the class.

Subsequent lesson: Tell a student, privately, the time that she is to show the class (using her hands). Have the class respond by naming the time she shows.

Robbis was told, "You're a clock; set your hands at 8:30 so someone facing you can tell the time." Then the class answered the question, "What time is it?"

Note: When students use their bodies to demonstrate time, the exercise works better with hours, quarter-hours, and half-hours. We found that students watching the demonstration often disagree about the time shown at intermediate positions.

> ***Variation:*** Following this activity, tell a student, "You're a clock; set your hands." Don't specify the time. Ask students facing her: "What time is it?"

> ***Benefit:*** The physical activity required for the response helps keep students alert, and helps them internalize the words.

Systematic drill: Students recite time in five-minute intervals: 5 after 9, 10 after 9, quarter after 9, etc. Then they do the same with another time-telling style: 9:05, 9:10, 9:15, etc.

Recapitulation: Each student has a sheet of paper with clocks drawn on it in rows, and scraps of paper the right size for covering one clock. The clocks are set at different times. A caller says the time of one of the clocks in the foreign language, using the 24-hour system if applicable.
If a student sees that she has that time on her board, she must repeat it in the foreign language to get permission to cover that clock with a

scrap of paper. The first student who covers the whole board or a designated portion thereof, such as one horizontal or vertical row, wins.

One student has found on her Bingo card three clock times that she heard the caller read aloud. She repeated the times and was given slips of paper to cover the clocks. If she is the first to cover four clocks in a horizontal row, she will win the game.

Intermittent reviews: Ask the time frequently in class, and tell certain students to ask you the time every 15 minutes.

> ***Benefits:*** Legitimizing clock-watching in our classes actually reduced the amount of time spent on it and harnessed some of that energy for learning.

Recycling with other topics: Command three students in a row: "Maria, wash your face at 7:00. Daniel, make a phone call at 10:30. Julie, eat lunch at 12:00." Set a paper-plate clock or point at a clock drawn on the board set at one of these times and the student whose time was indicated will pantomime.

USING CORRECT WORD ORDER

Make large flash cards, preferably 6x14 in size, containing words and phrases that can be combined into a few basic sentences. Have a group of students stand in front of the class and hold the cards up so that they form a sentence that you say aloud. The students who are watching read the sentences aloud. Let them suggest new sentences or combinations. If necessary, they should direct the students into the correct position (in the foreign language).

Later, students themselves can unscramble sets of word cards that form a sentence. Physically moving the words or seeing them moved helps students remember word order rules. In some of our classes, students showed humor and creativity in using wastebaskets, lecterns, and chairs for punctuation or conjunctions.

Students create the sentence *Ich weiß, daß du mitkommst* 'I know that you're coming along' from a scrambled set of word cards. The rest of the class reads the sentence aloud. The student at the end is holding two cards: *mit* (a separable prefix) and *kommst* (a verb). Earlier he and the female student made a simple sentence, *du kommst mit* 'you're coming along.' Now they join a fellow student to create a complex sentence.

Variation: Focus on specific word order rules by setting up situations that require using them. In German, for instance, practice verb-second position by putting a card with an adverb such as "today" first and having students move the subject to third position; practice verb-last position by adding a subordinating conjunction and sending the verb to the end of the clause. By **physically moving** with their words, students internalize syntactical transformations.

4. Games by Technique

RESPONDING TO COMMANDS

These activities are organized into beginning and intermediate levels of language acquisition. They begin with easier, less complicated commands and move on to more difficult ones. The content for the commands can coincide with the structures and topics in the curriculum or can complement the curriculum.

Beginning Level

• Give students commands that help them **relax** or make them **more alert**, to perform activities such as calisthenics, yoga, marching, or dance.

• A student leaves the room and others hide something. When the student returns, the others direct the person to find the object: "Walk forward six steps; now turn to the left and go up to Harry's desk; look under it."

• Give a student a command and ask the class whether or not she is doing it. Tell her to deliberately carry out some commands incorrectly.

> ***Benefits:*** When students decide what erroneous command to act out, they exercise their creative faculties. If students do not understand a command, they are not put on the spot in front of the class. Fellow students are kept alert through their responsibility to evaluate the action.

• Students are "out" of the game if they obey a command not preceded by "Simon says," or without first asking "May I?"

> ***Variation:*** In a group of affirmative commands, occasionally give negative commands *(don't eat any apples, don't sit down);* students who perform the prohibited action are out of the game.

• Give a command and ask "**Possible or impossible?**" Mix possible and impossible commands. Later teach the construction "Can you...?" e.g., "Can you lie down on the floor and rub your ear on the ceiling?" Have students act out the possible commands. Examples of impossible commands: Bring me the chalkboard; touch your nose with your ear; hand Sally the floor.

Students enjoy arguing about whether or not a given action is really impossible. It is best to agree on some ground rules, e.g. that actions must be unaided by tools to qualify.

- Give each student a card with commands. They work in pairs, giving each other different commands.

- Take roll by giving each student a command to carry out or having them give you one. Or each student commands the next, in a chain reaction; you take roll as they respond.

- Give a command (*do something, move something, touch something,* etc.), then name two students who should carry it out. As they carry it out, tell the class what is being done. Then ask another student what the two are doing.

  Example: Move something, Troy and Bill! Troy is moving the wastebasket, and Bill is moving the flowers. What are they doing, Zulema?

- Students stand in pairs; the teacher gives commands involving interaction (*touch a shoulder, point at a toe);* all perform at once.

- Each student has a different list of things to do (could be matched with their interests or abilities), such as "Write down the name of someone present with two brothers" or "Find someone who will sing a foreign-language song with you." All work at once. If you want students to restrict themselves to the second language, you can make a rule that anyone heard speaking the first language is out of the game.

- Take an object such as a ball, and ask the class, "What shall I do with the ball?" Students then give you commands. Other students could take this role instead of you if you prefer. In this game students often ask the teacher to take the ball out of the room, put it in the wastebasket, bounce it ten times, or throw it out the window. Pantomiming is appropriate if it is not convenient to carry out the command exactly as it is given.

Variation: Ask a question using this shell: "How many times shall I ___?" For example, ask, "How many times shall I open this book?" A student answers with a full command, e.g., "Open the book three times."

Benefits: Students find games with commands more interesting with one complication, such as specifying when or a number of times; this allows you to use more complex sentence structure. For example, ask, "When shall I pick up the book?" A student answers, "Pick up the book when I laugh."

- **Whisper** a command to a student, that student whispers it to another, and so on; the last student must perform the action, and the teacher reports whether or not the command was passed on accurately. This can be done with the intention of having it passed along accurately, or of having it whispered quickly and indistinctly so that the end result is humorous.

- **Dictate** to the class short letters or stories that use the commands that have been learned during the semester. Pause occasionally for students to suggest some commands to include.

    Benefits: In our college classes, this exercise served as a good review and captured the interest of the students. Occasionally, students who want to write a letter to native-speaker friends or relatives will allow their letter to become a class project.

- **Combine** commands to create detailed instructions for a complicated task such as making a phone call, driving a car, writing and mailing a letter, or getting up and dressing.

    Example: Open the car door, get in, sit down, and take the key from your purse or pocket. Sometimes let students figure out what the individual commands produce (take a pencil, touch the paper with the pencil, move your hand to the left, down, to the right, up; that's a square).

Intermediate Level

- Students choose something they know how to do well and with the aid of vocabulary provided by the teacher prepare a **demonstration** for the class: "Take a needle. Put the thread through the hole. Pull the thread."

- Students, in pairs or in front of the class, give each other commands using only verbs from a story they have read. The funnier, the better, since vocabulary practiced in a novel context is remembered better. The commands need not retell the story, but students should restrict themselves to verbs from the story.

  > *Variation:* The teacher or other students describe the actions that were carried out, in the **present** or **past** tense. This offers a second review of the story vocabulary.

  > *Variation:* One student directs several others through a short reenactment of the story, using commands.

- **Complicated commands with conditional sentences:**
  Michelle, if your book is open, close it, and if it is already shut, open it.
  Peter, if another student has a cap, offer him your cap and ask him for his. If he says no, leave your cap with him and go back to your chair."

GUESSING

Guessing games can begin as soon as students have learned a small repertoire of descriptive adjectives, fundamental verbs, and nouns for common objects. This usually means the second half of the first-year secondary school classes and the second half of the first-semester college classes.

Ways of handling guessing

- One statement at a time is made about a person, place, or thing being guessed, with a pause after each statement for guessing.

- Guessers use adjectives from a list on the board. (*Is it a _____ object?*) We have found that the game moves faster if question cues appear on the board. Possible adjectives: triangular, square, round, flat, expensive, delicious, colorful, cheap, fashionable.

- Guessers might ask only questions that can be answered *yes* or *no*. At other times, they might ask for specific information, such as "Why do you like it?" "What day of the week does it come on?"

- Especially at higher levels, guessers can set a scene (*it's raining in the forest,* for example) and ask "What do you say?" If the thing being guessed is a cat, the answer might be, "I don't like for my fur to get wet." If it is a mushroom, the answer could be, "This will help me grow and be healthy."

What can be guessed

- *What word am I?* Students identify vocabulary words, based on definitions or clues the teacher gives, pausing after each clue as class guesses what it is. By guessing they can win points for their team. Example: "It is a vehicle that takes more than 200 people very rapidly from one city to another on rails." Answer: "A train."

   Variation: Have a student lead the activity after offering the person a list of possible things to be guessed or a set of pictures representing them.

   Variation: The class chooses something to be guessed by one to six students who are out of the room. When they return, they take turns trying to guess it. Class members take turns answering the guesses.

- *Who, where, what am I?* Names, occupations, and famous tourist attractions might be guessed in this activity.

   Variation: The student giving clues must include a proper noun from the category in question in his answer.

   Examples: Is it a city? No, it's not New York. Or: Yes, but it's not St. Louis.
   Is it a mountain? No, it's not Mount Rushmore. Or: Yes, but it's not Mount Rainier.

- *What am I thinking of?* Where is the ___ hidden? Where am I going to put this ___?

- *What's in my pocket (in the sack)?* Show possible objects first.

   Variation: Cover objects with a single sheet of newspaper and let students feel them.

- *To whom does it belong?* Students put one object from their pocket or purse in a bag. Then objects are drawn and students guess owners one at a time, giving reasons why they think that person is the owner. Here it helps to remind students to make **simple sentences**, using **familiar vocabulary**.

- *What's out of place?* A student leaves the room; objects are put in strange places; the student returns, and figures out and explains which items are out of place.

  > *Variation:* The class decides how many oddities a student should be able to identify and describe in, say, two minutes. If the student succeeds in doing so in a comprehensible manner, a reward may be given. This activity is reserved for the few minutes remaining at the end of class.

  > *Benefits:* Enjoyable way to internalize prepositional phrases used in everyday language.

While one student was out of the room, the other students made things as topsy-turvy as possible. The student came back in and explained in the foreign language as many things as he could that were wrong with the room.

- *Which student am I?* A member of the class is described by the teacher or another student. She is to say, "That's me!" when she recognizes herself from the clues. This game can be played at all levels. Intermediate and advanced students can write brief autobiographical sketches from which the teacher selects details as clues for the game.

- *What am I doing?* Each student is given a card with a verb or phrase to pantomime; others guess what they are doing. The first to guess correctly does the next pantomime. Students at all levels enjoy winning points for their team by pantomiming something that their team guesses. If their team fails to guess, the other team gets a chance.

   Variation: Teams prepare pantomimes for the other team to guess.

- *How am I doing it?* A student chooses an adverb from a long list of adverbs on the board and pantomimes or does something. The class guesses *how* he is doing it, i.e., which adverb applies.

- *How does the story go?* Read aloud sentences or paragraphs from stories or dialogues with which students are familiar. Ask where it is, who is speaking, what just happened, and what object is being described.

   Variation: Teacher or students make up descriptions of the location, person, thing, or event from the story and others guess who or what is being described.

SIMULATING

Simulations are appropriate for **all levels** of acquisition and lend themselves well to almost all of the topics or themes in the course curriculum. If the curriculum is not topic or theme-centered, teachers will need to prepare students in advance by teaching pertinent vocabulary and structures.

Places in a city: Label parts of the room with signs, using the chalkboard as well. Then send students to various locations and ask them where they are going, who's already there, what they can do there, etc.

Lisa and Scott answer questions about the stores and buildings in their make-believe German town.

At the restaurant: Four students are given menus and take turns giving orders for meals to the entire class, who are waiters and write down the orders. The correct orders are written on the board by the teacher so students can check their work. Use food pictures or artificial food, plastic dishes, etc., if possible.

> *Variation:* Table-setting instructions are used to practice position and direction terms. Instructors find it helpful to give students commands to **un-set** the table as well; they can put all plates in a stack, all forks in one box, etc.

Shopping: Students ask how much, compare prices, and tell the clerk what they want. A proprietor or clerk (role-played by teacher initially) gets things from the shelf for students; students put items in their own shopping bags. Students pay and receive change with play money.

> *Variation:* Before the simulated shopping game that was just described, the class is divided into groups of four; each group is given the name of a kind of store. Cards, each bearing the name of something one can buy at a store, are mixed and laid out for each group. The four students choose appropriate cards to stock their store and go to a corner of the room to "set up shop." A simulated

buying game follows. One student in each group remains as clerk, and the others shop in other stores.

Variation: Students bring "white elephants" (unwanted garage sale items) and set them up in "departments" (as in stores) labeled with signs. Students actually buy and sell those objects they no longer want with the money issued to them by the "bank" and then take their purchases home to keep.

Variation: After playing the "white elephant" variation, our students asked for and received permission to play it again as an auction. They bid so high on each other's "white elephants" that they practiced numbers which were not normally used in classroom games. They spoke with more complicated syntax than usual in the attempt to explain why they wanted particular items or why they did not mind when another student was the highest bidder.

Benefits: This is one of the most popular games. It takes an entire period to play and can be used to review several weeks' vocabulary and structures. Students also enjoy cutting out mimeographed play money to help prepare for the game.

At the office: One student, playing boss, dictates a letter on a subject of genuine interest to another student, playing secretary, who takes notes and then writes out the letter in the foreign-language business letter format and presents it to the "boss" for approval. Then they exchange roles or change partners.

Pen pals: Each student writes a letter to a student in another foreign-language class at the same or a higher level and receives an answer, which is shared with the class.

News reports: Assign student "reporters" to attend a free museum exhibit, movie, concert, dance, play, or watch a TV show and report on it as a TV reviewer or in the form of a newspaper review.

Variation: A bulletin board in the classroom serves as a newspaper. Sections change as students contribute new items. The teacher edits the items; some of the items could be recorded on cassettes for a "radio program" and "broadcast" to the class or another class.

Familiar stories: Students pantomime actions from a story they have read. The teacher reads a summary or the entire story while all or some of the students pantomime. People can take the parts of inanimate objects to some extent to increase the number of participants. The story can be the description of a **simple action** such as **driving** somewhere or **phoning**, composed and duplicated by the teacher for the class.

> *Variation:* Students **improvise skit versions** of the story.

> *Variation:* In pairs in front of the class, students conduct a **mock interview** in which one student plays a character from a familiar story and the other a reporter, policeman, or future employer interviewing her. The interviewer tells the class his conclusions about the character.

Unfamiliar stories: Guide students through acting out an unfamiliar story by using directed dialogue along with commands for actions:
Tell a student: "Say that you bought the radio yesterday."
To another student: "Ask him where he bought it."
To the first student: "Look around nervously and tell her to stop asking you questions."
After acting out the story, students listen to it read aloud and then read it themselves.

> *Benefits:* This kind of guidance helps students internalize vocabulary through action, and makes the plot and setting of the story clearer, which in turn increases comprehension while reading.

Other possibilities: Job interview; planning a trip at travel agency; going somewhere in a car (bus, plane...) and doing something when they get there; accepting an invitation and going to a party; buying a ticket and boarding a plane or train; getting up, going to bed; phone call; receiving visitors; gas station; doctor; post office; asking someone out on a date.

LISTING

Listing can be done individually, in pairs, or as a group (each contributing an item), either with or without a reference list of words from which to choose. Reference lists can consist of pictures or words. The game can be in the form of a question chain drill (*I'm going to Mexico during the vacation; where are you going?*), or students can supply single words or phrases in response to questions from the teacher. Here are some suggested categories in which students can make lists:

Visual cues

- All terms for parts of the classroom (such as walls) and objects in the classroom

- All objects of a certain kind in a picture

- The world around us: buildings, parts of a house (based on a city map or house picture)

- Possible places where an object might be hidden in the classroom (Various students can later be told to look in the places on the list.)

Vocabulary

- The seasons, months, days of the week, times of day (Students find this a reassuringly easy activity and are usually well prepared.)

- All nouns or adverbs that can be used with a certain verb

- Grocery lists, shopping lists, Christmas or birthday wish lists (Students could use mail-order catalogs in the foreign language.)

    Variation: First student says, "I'm going shopping today and I'm going to buy a _____." Students must repeat what was said by students before them as well as their own contribution to the list. If they fail to do so, they are out of the game.

- Jobs and professions

- Items needed for preparing a dish, playing a sport, etc.

Personal information

- Students' daily or weekly schedules

- Specified number of animals in order of preference

- What they do when they get up in the morning (turn off alarm, wash face, etc.)

- What they would pack if they were going to a foreign country and could take just one suitcase

    Variations: "I'm going on a trip to Paris. I'm packing a suitcase. I'm taking _____." "In my store I sell _____." "They're loading the truck. With what? With _____." "For my birthday I would like _____." "I'm a famous inventor and I invented the _____."

- Favorite sports and games, musical instruments, kinds of music, hobbies

- Family relationships, listed in the form of a family tree, with names of relatives written in where possible and foreign-language words for father, mother, etc.

- What students would do if they won a million dollars (a long list); a hundred dollars

Reading passages

- All the words in a story they are reading that fit in a particular category: school, science, politics, food, car parts, etc.

    Variation: Students can be given foreign-language magazines and asked to search for words in a certain category throughout their magazine.

- All words in a reading passage that are necessary (or unnecessary) for a general understanding of the main point of the passage.

    Benefit: In our experimental program this helped students learn to read for meaning instead of translating.

Variations: All cognates or compound words in a reading passage; all time phrases and clues to time in a reading passage.

- All the places where they could look for something lost or hidden in a story, or all possible motives the suspects in a detective story might have.

- Students go to the board, and list words in certain categories from a given reading passage. They list at least one related word, one word that is part of a word family (with at least one other word from the family), one compound word, one word with its antonym, and one word or phrase with its synonym or another way of expressing it.

CATEGORIZING

In categorizing activities, the words that students list are subdivided according to a specified classification.

Feminine vs. masculine: Tell students to look around the room and name all the things they see that are masculine nouns and all that are feminine (and neuter if applicable).

Possible vs. impossible: The teacher gives a series of mixed possible and impossible commands or statements and asks students "Possible or impossible?"

> *Variation:* The teacher supplies the grammatical terms *question, statement,* and *command* as labels, and students say the correct label for each sentence read aloud by the teacher. Inserting several unusual commands or statements increases the memorability of the terms.

Reading comprehension: Based on stories or essays, students list what Mr. Jones does vs. what he thinks or says, what old people tend to do vs. what young people tend to do, positive and negative aspects of Carla's character, or examples of environmental pollution vs. environmental protection.

> *Benefit:* This is one of the best ways of encouraging students to focus on important aspects of a passage instead of translating.

Functions: Categorize a list of animate or inanimate objects by a common list of functions they can perform. List the functions on the board and have students categorize objects and describe the categorizations in brief sentences.

Example: "A person, a motor, and water can run."

F U N C T I O N S

		swim	ache	flow	run
O	person	√	√		√
B					
J	water			√	√
E					
C	motor				√
T					
S	stomach		√		

New Year's resolutions: Divide them into categories of usually kept vs. not usually kept, or realistic vs. unrealistic.

Leisure-time activities: Contrast vacation activities with weekend activities; contrast what they have done during a vacation with what they would ideally do.

Body parts: Categorize parts of the body as those of which humans have one vs. more than one. Humans have **one** head, mouth, nose, heart, stomach, back, but they have **two** ears, hands, lips, legs, etc.

Furniture: Separate furniture or other items according to the room of a house in which they belong.

Clothing: Classify articles of clothing by the part of the body on which they are worn, by places to which one can wear them, or by the weather or season in which they are worn.

Transportation: Categorize by air, land, and sea.

Desert island: Categorize what one might take to a desert island (food, drink, tools, entertainment, clothing); set some limits on quantity or space.

Food: List items in main food categories; health vs. junk food; cold- vs. hot-weather food, etc.

Meals: Students list what they like most to eat for each meal, compared with what might be eaten at the same meal by people in a country where the language is spoken.

Reading selections: Give students terms such as *dialogue, anecdote, letter, report, recipe,* and have them classify the texts that they have read so far in the semester.

Geography: Students classify a list of locations as cities, rivers, or mountain ranges in countries where the target language is spoken, or as countries bordering on these countries. For students of German who are given the list "Frankreich, Hameln, Schwarzwald, Bremen, Weser, Rhein, Harz, Polen," the students would write:
Cities: Bremen, Hameln
Rivers: Weser, Rhein
Mountain Ranges: Schwarzwald, Harz
Border Countries: Polen, Frankreich

Bingo game: The teacher gives students seven categories of words with which they have been working and they draw Bingo squares, seven down and seven across, and put the names of the seven categories above the seven squares across. Students fill in the boxes as quickly as possible. When time is up the teacher reads aloud from a master list of words in the category. Students who have an entire row consisting of words read out by the teacher or equally acceptable words win a prize.

> *Variation:* Bingo is played with names, nouns, titles, symbols, etc., in the squares instead of numbers. Phrases describing these items are read aloud (e.g., German physicist who developed the formula $E = mc^2$). The first student to mark off a row across or down wins.

Board game: Students form two teams. For each item put several related categories on the board, e.g., fruits, vegetables, meats. Students take turns supplying words for them, until each category has a minimum number of items. The team that has the most words listed accurately under appropriate columns after a designated period of time wins.

Celebrities: Students vote for celebrities whom they would like to meet. The instructor puts the top five on the board, and class takes turns describing their appearance, personality, or skills with words from a list on the board.

Animal descriptions: Names of eight zoo animals are written on the board at the heads of columns. Students take turns contributing adjectives to the lists under the names. One student pulls each column together by making complete-sentence descriptions of the animal in that column.

Pictures: Give students two or three categories of opposites such as weak vs. strong, hot vs. cold, and let them sort picture cards or words from a list into the categories.

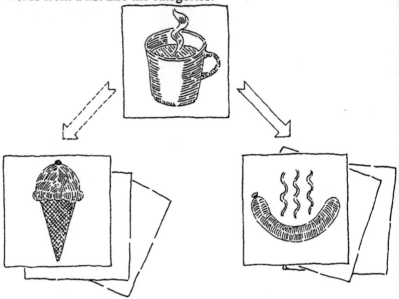

As students put flashcards into piles of hot and cold things, they describe the cards, e.g., "This is a cup of hot chocolate. It is hot." When they finish categorizing the cards orally, they will each write foreign-language lists of all words under the category labels *hot* and *cold*.

> **_Variation:_** Have students prepare flashcards of items *associated* with hot or cold instead of items that *are* hot or cold, e.g., an ice skate, a sand bucket with shovel, or a bag of charcoal. Use these in a categorizing activity such as the one above.

MATCHING

Here students connect two elements that belong together. This is one of the students' favorite vocabulary-building exercises.

- Students match new vocabulary words with definitions in the foreign language.

- Students match needs to the place where that need can be satisfied.

    Examples: Where do you go when you are ill?
                  To the doctor.
                  Where do you go if you need stamps?
                  To the post office.

- Match devices and machines to their uses.

    Examples: What do we use a refrigerator for?
                  To keep food cool.
                  What do we use a stove for?
                  To heat up our food.

- Match foreign and domestic holidays with the dates on which they are celebrated.

    Example: Valentine's Day: February 14th

- Match clothing with occasions.

    Examples: tuxedo: junior/senior prom
                  suit: job interview

- List 25-50 nouns on the board representing animals and 12 motion verbs. The teacher or students match them, making statements such as, "Pigeons crawl." Students reply: "Yes, pigeons crawl" or "No, that's wrong. Pigeons fly," whichever is true.

ASSOCIATING

Games involving the associating of one concept with another activate a student's imagination. This is one of their greatest benefits, since it encourages inference, which plays such a crucial role in comprehension.

Related words: Students match native-language words with foreign-language cognates or borrowed words, which may not mean the same as the native-language word, competing as in a spelling bee to win points for their teams.

 Example: livre - library

Word families: The teacher designates a basic word as "head" of the word family, such as the dictionary entry form or the simplest form of the main verb in the family. Students supply other members of the family, perhaps with sentence description clues from the teacher.

 Example: For the word family *work,* the teacher might give these clues: "A person who works *(worker);* a handout to write on *(worksheet);* household chores *(housework)."*

Compound words: The teacher says a compound word and students try to make more compound words using the parts of the word.

 Example: baseball: ballpoint pen, ballgown, highball, baseboard.

 Variation: The teacher gives students a compound word such as *homework* and they make a chain of words in which each begins with the last half of the previous compound word, e.g. *workbook, bookshelf, shelfpaper.*

 Note: Compound word games work better with languages that have a tendency to form compound words frequently, such as Germanic languages.

Pictures: Students make a quick rough sketch representing the word or sentence read aloud by the teacher, instead of writing it down.

 Benefit: Many of our students showed unsuspected talents (either drawing skill or imagination) and felt more encouraged to participate in class thereafter.

Common elements: Students are given a list of pictures or words containing items such as these: bottle, glass, cup, corner. Students figure out how three of the words are associated and mark out the one that doesn't belong.

Opposites: Students supply opposites of words given them by the teacher, as in a spelling bee. This is another of those tasks that students find reassuring and are eager to prepare for, like learning seasons, months, and days of the week.

> *Variations:* Students *do* instead of *say* the opposite; or a student says a word and points to someone who will say the opposite.

Synonyms and circumlocutions: The teacher gives a word; students supply synonyms or other ways of communicating the same idea or definitions. This works especially well when the teacher has chosen words for which synonyms have already appeared in the students' active vocabulary lists.

Descriptions: The teacher gives students pairs of words that are in some way comparable and asks students to use a logical adjective to compare them in a complete sentence.

> *Example:* sofa/chair: "A sofa is larger than a chair."

Stream of consciousness: A student says a word; in a chain drill, other students say a word of which they are reminded by the previous word. They could preface it by the phrase "That reminds me of...." They must be able to justify the logical association (in their native language).

> *Variation:* To make the game more competitive for higher levels, have the class stand. Allow students to challenge a fellow student's word choice by saying, "I don't see any connection." At this point, the student must explain the connection comprehensibly in the foreign language or else sit down. If he can do so convincingly, the challenger must sit down.

Competitive game: Divide the class into two teams. Both teams listen to a list of words that are related in some way. The first team to guess the relationship and express it comprehensibly in the foreign language wins a point.

> *Example:* popcorn, tickets, velvet curtains, a lion, cartoons (things you might see in a movie theater).

SEQUENCING

Putting story events into sequence is a technique that can be used with beginning students after about six weeks of instruction and continued through the advanced levels. Vocabulary should be familiar or the meanings possible to infer. The simplest version of this game is listed first, the most complex last.

- Students **put into order** scrambled events from a story they have already read (later, from one they haven't read).

    Benefit: This is another good way to encourage students to focus on reading for the main idea rather than translating.

- Students draw up a character's **daily schedule** or list of activities from time clues in a story they have read or from scrambled sentences.

- Give students **illogical sequences** *(It was freezing cold outside. I put my bathing suit on and rushed down to the water.)* and have them put the sentences in logical sequence or alter them so that they make sense.

- Students **list** everything in a story they are reading that happened in the past; then in the present; then what is predicted for the future.

- The teacher **reads aloud** one paragraph of a fairy tale each day, while students draw a rough sketch of what they understand. When the entire story has been read, give them a printed version with scrambled paragraphs and have them cut and paste paragraphs into an order that will tell a coherent story. This can be done with the aid of notes taken by the students as well as with drawings.

    Benefit: Our students were better able to focus on listening to the fairy tale because they had to draw what they heard.

    Variation: Initial reading is also in scrambled order. This makes the task more challenging.

- From a list of places to which an imaginary person wants to go, students **plan a route** that will take that person there in a logical and energy-saving sequence. (In a later week, introduce details such as deadlines that will complicate the planning.)

  Use as a basis either the school or college campus and nearby surroundings, or maps. Students can compose a travel itinerary for the imaginary person, with means of transportation and sights to see (preferably in the countries where the foreign language being studied is spoken).

5. Games Using Special Materials

OBJECTS

It is useful to keep these objects and materials on hand in a foreign language classroom, or in separate bags ready to be carried in:

- towels, toothpaste, toothbrushes, combs

- paper-plate clocks

- grab bag or box

- frisbees and foam-rubber balls

- play money, tickets, newspapers, menus

- food pictures stapled to cards and paper plates, or toy food such as plastic eggs

- food boxes, cans, packages (empty and clean)

- plastic glasses, cups, utensils, paper napkins, paper plates

- stuffed animals, colored building blocks, doll house with furniture, toy vehicles

- colored pencils and crayons of different lengths, colored paper

- old, large articles of clothing such as hats, boots, jackets, robes, gloves, fans, coats, aprons, jewelry, sunglasses

  Benefit: We have found it easy to use these objects in filler review games when there was unexpected free time in the class, such as when audiovisual equipment failed to work or a planned exercise did not work as well as expected.

Game 1. The teacher holds up an object and says, "This is a _____, yes or no?" Or, "Is this a _____?"

Variation: The teacher does something with an object but says she is doing it with a different object. Or, she does something different with the same object. She asks the class questions such as these:

"I'm picking up **the eraser**. True or false?"

"I'm **cleaning** the eraser. True or false?"

Game 2. The teacher holds up an object or performs an action with it and gives a choice: "Is that a pen or a pencil?" or "Am I writing on the board or erasing the board?"

Variation: The teacher asks the group to confirm an answer of an individual student, who is allowed to answer truthfully or deceitfully. The teacher asks, "Are you sitting or standing?" A student who is sitting answers, "Standing." The class says, "That's wrong."

Game 3. The teacher holds up an object and says "What is this?" Students recall the name of the object without prompting.

Game 4. The teacher holds up objects and names each in turn, then covers them with newspaper and asks the class to recall and write down the names of as many objects as possible.

Variation: A student feels objects through a newspaper or with eyes closed while naming them.

Game 5. The teacher hides or scatters various objects in the room and gives each student a list of them. For beginners, the list should contain all the scattered objects plus some others that are definitely not in the room. They check each object off as they see it. Advanced beginners match listed locations on a sheet with listed objects on the sheet. Intermediate students write sentences describing the location of the objects.

Game 6. The teacher holds up an object and asks students what one does with it or asks them to describe it. They give one-word answers (verb infinitives or color adjectives).

Game 7. Hold up pairs of similar objects and ask "What kind of _____ are these?" Students answer with an adjective such as *long*. With **beginning students**, answers can be colors or size descriptions. With **intermediate groups**, use a variety of adjectives such as: glass, plastic, wooden, metal, modern, old-fashioned.

Benefits: This is an entertaining review and recycling activity that taps student creativity and can be adapted to all levels.

Game 8. Ask students to take objects from a bag or remove items from their purses or pockets and name them. Then ask them to do certain things with them, e.g., to put them under the desk, to describe them with simple adjectives, or to say what one does with them, using verb infinitives. In our classes students enjoyed showing their possessions.

> *Variation:* Assign students to bring an old object that they have saved and explain why they have saved it. In one class this was the favorite activity of the year; students prepared long, elaborate explanations.

Game 9. A different object is passed down each row. The second student asks the first what it is. The third asks the second and is told, "Jack says it's a hat." The fourth student is told, "Jack and Hortensia say it's a hat." The game starts again in the next row.

Game 10. A student closes her eyes. Another student hides something. The first student opens her eyes and asks questions such as: "Is it near or far?" The other student answers and gives her clues as needed. The student in each pair that finds the other's hidden object with the fewest questions and clues is the winner.

Game 11. The teacher throws a foam rubber ball to someone and asks, "What are you doing?" **Answer:** "I'm catching the ball."

Teacher: "What am I doing?"
Student: "You're throwing the ball."

Teacher: "What is he doing?"
Student: "He's catching the ball."

Teacher: "What are you saying?"
Student: "I'm saying that he's catching the ball."

> *Benefits:* This technique is adaptable to many verbs and syntactic structures. (See the section on Describing Actions, in Chapter 3: Games by Learning Category.)

Game 12. Students say which objects in the room belong to whom. Give students an opportunity to show recognition of appropriate **possessive adjectives** as you point and say: "Is that **his** or **her** book?" Then let them answer w-questions calling for possessive adjectives: "Whose book is that?" Answer: "That's **your** book."

Game 13. Bring small packages and bottles with spices and other seasonings. Give class a list of the foreign-language names of these seasonings and have them look at and smell them. Later, change the order on the list and number the seasonings. Have students write the name by the number for each seasoning on the basis of its appearance and smell.

Note: At an **intermediate level**, it is best to use high-frequency ingredients such as salt, sugar, baking soda, pepper, garlic, vanilla, tomato sauce, chili powder, mayonnaise, sour cream, mustard, catsup, or cinnamon.

Game 14. With toy cars and buses, tiny dolls and animals, doll furniture, and perhaps a doll house, tell students to drive cars in certain directions, furnish a room in the house (e.g., "Put the chair next to the bed"), etc. This activity works best with small classes (or, if there are enough sets of materials, with small groups).

> *Variation:* Ask students in what direction the cars should go, in what room a piece of furniture belongs, etc.

> *Benefit:* This is ideal as a **recycling activity** for **intermediate-level groups** because it incorporates so much vocabulary.

Game 15. Students dramatize or pantomime stories, perhaps folk tales familiar to all, or stories the class has read, with stuffed animals or puppets as actors.

Game 16. Organize a treasure hunt with clues leading to other clues. The final clue leads to the treasure.

> *Variation:* With the class divided into several small groups, have each group write clues to a treasure hunt. The clues can be corrected and then recorded on separate slips of paper. The next day, the teacher quickly tapes the clues where they belong and each group embarks on a treasure hunt prepared by a different group.

Sample series of clues: Without me you can't leave class. You can write better if you use me. I'm often dirty and I'm near something green. The treasure is under something the teacher uses at the beginning of class.

AUTHENTIC PROPS

Calendars: Display a large calendar or distribute duplicated calendars. Have students figure out on which day of the week various holidays and their own birthdays fall and say the name of the day of the week as well as the date.

Menus: Using a menu, students pair up and take turns being waiter or guest in a restaurant and ordering food and drink.

> *Variation:* Teacher has students analyze the menu, asking them: What is the cheapest main dish? What should I order if I'm very hungry and have only ____ (some small amount in the foreign currency)?

Travel schedules: Give students train timetables. Ask them when a train leaves a specific city for another city.

> *Variation:* Ask students to plan the quickest, cheapest, or most convenient train trip between two cities on the basis of timetables.

Country maps. Give students a country map and have them plan a trip involving four cities, telling the class: "We're going from Köln to Berlin to Frankfurt to Hamburg." Class members trace the route on the map.

Later, hand out a map with numbers instead of names of cities (countries, famous sights, etc.), and have them recall as many names as they can and write them in. Without going over answers, proceed to make statements like, "We're going from #1 to #7," to which the class replies, "We're going from Köln to Berlin." Students may correct or write in the city names next to the numbers.

> *Benefit:* Students learn locations actively through physical contact with the map; they learn from listening to the answers given by their peers.

Students point out the location of various buildings in Hamburg on a map of the city and discuss the best route from one place to the next.

> *Variation:* Write a list of cities on the board. Show students the cities on a map, saying "Bremen is northwest of Munich," etc. Then point at the two cities again, say a student's name, and ask the person to express the geographical relationship.

City maps and layouts: Students are given a simplified map of a typical foreign city, with streets and principal public buildings labeled. The teacher tells the students several places they need to go and asks them in what street these places are and where they should go first if they are starting at the train station.

> *Variation 1:* The teacher says where students should start on the map and gives directions for them to get to another place on their duplicated maps. They trace the route in pencil and tell him where he's sent them (to a bakery) and what they can do there (buy bread).

> *Variation 2:* The teacher starts students at the train station and gives them directions without telling them where they will end up. At the end she asks them where they have arrived.

Variation 3: After students have heard the teacher give directions several times, the teacher tries a new version. He says where he is and where he wants to go on his shopping trip; students direct him there. Then he asks for an alternate route or a more efficient, shorter route, or a scenic route.

Variation 4: Duplicate simplified maps of students' own city. In small groups, students tell each other how to get from the school to their own homes.

Note: This activity can be done without props, also. As one student explains how to get from school to her home, another student draws a rough map of the directions on the board.

Authentic forms and applications: A student fills out a form such as a job application with the aid of the teacher or another student who asks her questions. The student who is helping may be given a list of questions corresponding to the items on the application.

Magazines, newspapers, brochures: Give students periodicals or brochures. Assign them "research projects" to answer questions on a list or to find as many words as possible in a certain semantic field, such as politics or entertainment, in these magazines.

Sample project: Find out which movie stars made a new film this year.

Benefits: The "research projects" help students focus on reading for the main idea, and the word-finding projects help convince them that they can figure out the general meanings of many words they have never seen before. Students acquire a more realistic impression of the target culture by looking at pictures and ads and the general topics treated.

Signs and symbols: Make handwritten signs on large cards, such as **EXIT, ONE-WAY STREET, CLOSED TODAY.** Point to a sign and ask a student what he should do or expect when he sees it.

CARDS

Physical response props. Objects students need to manipulate during physical response commands can be represented by **words** or **pictures** on **cards:** Give Mary the hat (represented by card); put the keys (card) next to the purse (card).

Command pictures and labels. Students in pairs are given **cards** picturing actions with commands written on them. One partner gives a command from a card and watches to see if the other is carrying out the command correctly.

Matching picture and sentence cards. Students **match sentence cards** or **word cards** with appropriate **pictures.** Sentence or word cards could be given to half the class and picture cards matching these to the other half. Students find the appropriate matching card by showing their card and looking at others' cards.

> *Variation:* Students match synonyms or antonyms by finding another student with the other half of the pair.

Simulations. Use cards to represent places or objects: e.g., a restaurant simulation in which people fill their plates with cards that represent food.

"Go Fish" card game. Make your own "Go Fish" games by collecting four pictures in a number of categories, such as clothing, from magazines. Cards are shuffled and seven cards are dealt to each player. Each player can ask the person on his left for a card he needs to complete a set of four, saying, for instance, "Do you have any insects?" If the player does have one, he gives it up only if the first player can identify it correctly ("It's a fly."). The first player draws from the pile of leftover cards if the second player does not have the card asked for.

Examples of sets: drinks, fruits, plants, mammals, insects, silverware, tools.

Note: So that several smaller groups can play, make a number of different decks of cards.

> *Benefits:* Students learn vocabulary by associating members of a category.

Sentence building. Give each student a card with a word or phrase on it. Direct several students into formation so that the cards they hold up **form a sentence.** Have another student read the sentence. Add an adverb at the beginning (to force word order shifts in German) or insert a conjunction to form a compound sentence. By moving physically to make necessary word order changes, students internalize transformations.

Or, substitute a verb or preposition for one in the original sentence and have a student with a new noun or pronoun come up and insert herself in an appropriate position to replace another student so that the sentence makes sense.

Humor as well as clear breaks between sentences or clauses can be introduced by using wastebaskets, lecterns, etc., as periods and commas.

Note: This game is especially useful with languages that have strict rules for word order.

> *Variation:* Students can make up their own sentences and direct each other to go into formation with the cards.

> *Variation:* The teacher can say sentences and students can go into formation on their own.

> *Variation:* Students can make words with letter cards, form opposites of words just made, or form adjectives to modify nouns just made.

Parts of speech shapes. Give students cards with words on them. Those in the **shape of arrows** are **verbs**; those that are **oval** are **nouns** or **pronouns** (**color-coded** for case in languages where objects have a different form from subjects). Deal out nouns and have students draw verbs. **Prepositions** could be **squares,** and **conjunctions** could be **diamonds.**

Each group of four students should have a complete deck of ten or twenty sentences' worth of cards. They can build and add to each other's sentences. The group with the most valid sentences at the end of the allotted time wins.

A group of five students is given a set of fifty or so cards. They confer briefly and put together their first sentence, *Wir fahren an den See* (We're going to the lake).

Visuals for vocabulary chain games. Each student has a **picture card** representing some kind of food. The first student says "I went to the market and I bought some ...." The second student repeats the sentence, adding the food pictured on her card. Each student repeats the entire sentence and adds her item.

> *Variation:* (for **intermediate levels**) "I'm going to make a cake. I'll put in some...." Or, "I took a ride in my car but had problems with everything: the door; the windshield wipers; the oil; the gas..."

Interview cue cards. With questions written on index cards as cues, have students ask each other conversational or interview questions, take notes on the answers, and be prepared to describe each other to the class.

> *Variation:* Write a question and its answer on each card. The cards are passed around the room, each student taking one. The first student asks his neighbor the question on his card so that the whole class can hear it. If she answers correctly, she gets to keep the card. She proceeds to ask her other neighbor the question on her own card. If he answers incorrectly, the card is passed to his neighbor, who proceeds to ask *her* other neighbor the same question. The cards keep going around until they are answered. The student with the most cards (and thus the most correct answers) wins.

Adapting board games. Advanced students can adapt commercial geography board games, on each turn either moving to a new city or planning entertainment for the city they are in.

With reference books such as train timetables, menus, and travel guides at hand, the adapted game can introduce information about life in foreign countries as well as geography.

PICTURES

Yes or no? Point to a picture and say, "That's a dog, yes or no?" or "Is this a man?" Students answer "Yes" or "No."

> *Variation:* Students match numbered sentence cards or word cards to numbered pictures. For **beginners**, the pictures might depict simple activities such as a man playing the piano, a woman playing tennis, and a woman watching a play.
>
> As they read the sentences (e.g., "Sentence 1. She's watching a play. Sentence 2. She's playing tennis.") they identify Sentence 1 as describing Picture C, Sentence 2 as describing Picture B, and so on.
>
> *Variation:* Show, draw on board, or hand out three or four large duplicated pictures that are numbered. Describe the scene or action and have students identify the correct picture by number.

Here, intermediate students look at Pictures A, B, and C while the instructor reads aloud: "Sentence 1: The old man is taking a book from the young girl and talking to the old woman. Sentence 2: The young girl is sitting between her grandfather and her grandmother and is reading a book. Sentence 3: The old man is sitting between the young girl and the old woman." Students identify Sentence 1 as describing Picture B, Sentence 2 as Picture C, and Sentence 3 as Picture A.

What is this? Show a picture and ask what it is.

> *Variation:* Show a numbered set of two or three pictures, each differing by one attribute, and ask: "What kind of _____ is that? Which is larger? Which is newer, Picture 1, 2, or 3?"

> *Variation:* Show a set of three pictures, two of which are similar. Ask "Which is different?" Students name the different object.

Draw my description. Describe a person, action, object, or scene; have students draw a rough sketch with stick figures and perhaps label it.

> *Variation:* Have students draw pictures of word sets. A "year" is drawn as a line broken by seasons, the seasons in turn broken by months, with labels. A "family" is drawn as a family tree with names for types of relatives written in. A "town" is several square buildings, labeled. One of our liveliest teaching assistants used versions of this game over and over.

> *Benefit:* Teacher presents a model of how to make vocabulary review cards without using the native language.

Arrange the furniture. Draw on the chalkboard or overhead projector a simple house plan with several rooms. Ask students to "put the couch in the living room" and "move furniture" by erasing and redrawing the labeled squares.

Lisa and Scott are rearranging the living room furniture in this apartment, by erasing drawings of furniture and redrawing them in different positions.

Variation: Have students sort pictures of furniture and objects into "rooms of a house," or do the same with doll furniture and a doll house. The opportunity to choose how to furnish their own rooms seems to be inexhaustibly fascinating to students, so the more pictures available, the better.

Draw me a map. Give students directions in the foreign language and have them draw a map of how to get to their destination, with arrows and labels.

Food pictures. Use food pictures cut from magazines and **pasted on cards** to play restaurant or grocery store. Have students **sort pictures** into "meals" or use them as cues for the memory game "I went to my grandmother's house for dinner and I ate..." (in which all foods mentioned earlier are repeated as well as one's own contribution).

Compound words. Have a student draw a "word picture" for a compound word, such as a hand and a shoe for the German word *Handschuh,* meaning *glove;* other students identify the word.

> *Benefits:* This is particularly helpful in any language which has many compound words, since students need to learn to recognize them as made up of familiar parts.

Cartoons. Cut out a cartoon, if possible a cartoon strip, for each student and have them write the dialogue or a title or a descriptive sentence beneath each picture. Cartoons without words are best.

> *Benefits:* This activity gives students a chance to create with the language in a simple, enjoyable, personal way.

Art exhibits. Lay out pictures on a table or prop them in the chalk tray by the board to be an "art exhibit." They should be numbered. Students label them with a descriptive title and compare their list later with a list of the real titles. Then give students a vocabulary list and have them describe the pictures in greater detail.

> *Variation:* Intermediate students could label these pictures with creative titles. Later students hear the various titles and guess which picture they match.

Benefit: The same cards can be used in two different class preparations.

What's wrong in the picture? Duplicate copies of a drawing with several items drawn wrong, as in children's magazines, e.g., a chair with five legs. Have students write sentences describing each error they find.

Word pictures. Ask a student to pose for the class and have each student describe him with several sentences (a word "picture"). Attention should be given to the student's precise position as well as to his physical characteristics.

Note: This works especially well with intermediate students.

Jackie poses as a diver and Rick as a thinker, while their fellow students describe them with several sentences each.

Connect pictures to compose a story. A student pulls a picture from a large box full of pictures and begins a story based on something in the picture. When the first student stops, the next student takes a different picture and continues the story, incorporating something from the new picture in the story. The story continues until each student has contributed, or all pictures have been used.

Retell a story through pictures. Find magazine pictures or draw a series of stick-figure scenes on the chalkboard to use as cues and tell a story by referring to these illustrations. Then have students retell the story from these cues.

Pictures can also be used to practice structures, such as relative clauses describing someone in the picture. Each student identifies a character with a relative clause, e.g., "Bob is the man who always wears a hat." Another option is to imbed the relative clause in a question such as, "Who is the woman who smokes all the time?"

STORIES

Although your curriculum may already include reading selections, accumulating a variety of reading materials to complement it provides many opportunities for enrichment. The activities described here made their reading texts come alive for dozens of students in our experimental program.

Pantomiming. Students pantomime a **simple story** as the teacher tells or reads it, or they obey commands based on actions in the story. For example, the teacher reads, "Mr. Brown drinks his coffee," and commands students to pantomime drinking coffee. Later, students can present the story as a skit, saying a few essential phrases but relying mostly on actions.

Choosing the main idea. Students choose the **main idea** from a multiple-choice list: first after reading and hearing a story, and a few weeks later, after hearing the same story again.

Using advance organizers. Before reading a story aloud in class, help students guess who the main characters will be and what they will do and what questions about characters or events might be answered by the end of the story. Information used might be primarily pictures and titles in books, but in magazines, subtitles and captions are often available as advance organizers.

Finding key words. Students write down key words and phrases from a story or underline them on a duplicated story.

> _Variation:_ Students read a paragraph, close the book, write down the key words and phrases they remember, and compare their work with the book.

Remembering the facts. Read the class a short informative text, telling them ahead of time that they will be asked to remember two to five major facts. The class collectively contributes as many major facts as possible. The teacher notes them briefly on the board and keeps prodding and if necessary rereading until major facts are recalled.

Matching sentences to familiar stories. List by title on the board a number of stories students have read. Read aloud a random series of significant sentences chosen from various stories and have students indicate to which story they belong. Put a checkmark under that story's title.

Childhood stories which students read in English may be used here in the foreign language if students have enough vocabulary.

Telling what characters might say. Distribute and read aloud to students a story with dialogue, in which not all speakers are named. After students have read it once, re-read a line to them and ask, "Who's speaking?" Students should identify one (or perhaps more than one) possible speaker of each part in the dialogue. In our college classes some lively discussions were occasionally necessary to establish the most likely speaker.

> *Variation:* If quotations are not enclosed in quotation marks, have students pencil in the marks on the duplicated story. This shows whether or not they can tell when one speaker stopped and another started.

> *Variation:* After students have read a story, create new lines of dialogue for several of the characters, and have students tell you which characters would say the line, based on the context in which they appeared in the story. Or have students create new lines.

Identifying tenses. After students can recognize at least one past tense, have them go through a story containing that tense and some present and/or future tense forms and **label** the tense of all verbs.

Titling a story. Students read an **untitled story**, suggest titles for it, and vote on the best title. They can be asked to justify their choice.

Telling jokes. Give each student a slip of paper with a different joke. Ask them to learn the jokes by the next day.

Divide the class in half. One half stays seated in a semicircle. The other half moves around in the semicircle, taking turns telling their joke to each of the students in the first half. Then the two halves exchange roles. The class votes on the best-told joke.

Each student has memorized a different joke in Spanish. Half of the class moves around a semicircle telling the joke to each member of the other half. Soon the listeners will vote on the best joke.

Writing poems. Give students eight to ten common rhyming word pairs and have them write verses using as many of the words as possible (minimum four lines). If they prefer, allow them to draw a picture using the same concepts. Poems need not rhyme perfectly.

Solving a crime. Leave "clues" around the classroom. Give students a list of questions about the time and other circumstances of a hypothetical crime based on a detective story.

Have them walk around the room, **making notes** in the target language that answer questions on their list but leaving the clues untouched. When the time is up, the class discusses the crime and decides when and how it was committed and perhaps by whom.

> *Variation:* The class is told details of a crime and is told that two people in the class are "suspected"; but they were together, not near the scene of the crime, and thus have an alibi.
>
> The two students leave the room and spend five minutes making up the details of their alibi, return, and are questioned by the other students, who try to break down the alibi.

Turning stories into plays. Have students **adapt** a suitable story for dramatic presentation, retaining all dialogue and writing short passages for a narrator to read aloud where necessary.

Identifying similar meanings. Underline unusual or unfamiliar constructions in a story and have each student choose from a list a construction of similar meaning for each example. For example, a student who reads "If this be true" would mark "If that's the case."

Expanding a sentence into a story. The first student gives a short, simple sentence and each student contributes one word or phrase to expand it. For example: The cat chased the rat. The fat cat chased the rat. The fat cat chased the rat around the attic.

> *Variation:* Together the class tells an entire familiar story, or one they invent, in the following manner: The first student contributes a sentence, the second adds a sentence logically following the first, and so on.
>
> This activity can be used virtually every class day with different content and still capture the interest of the class and involve them in genuine communication.
>
> *Variation:* The teacher tells a story but stops frequently to ask the class to invent a detail: what the character is wearing, where she is going, etc. Students may also interrupt the teacher to ask detailed questions.

Telling and retelling stories. Four students leave the room. The class prepares to tell a brief story that is on a duplicated handout. One of the students returns and the class jointly tells him the story. Another returns and the first student tells that person the story. The second tells the third and the third student tells the fourth. At the end, the class corrects mistakes that may have slipped into the fourth version of the story.

6. Continuing with Games

As you begin to make up your own classroom games, you will probably want to write a brief description of each game on a 4 X 6 card and keep it in a file box on your desk along with cards describing your favorite games from this book. For an easy filing system, divide your games into alphabetized categories like the ones listed in the Table of Contents of this book.

Having a box of game descriptions at hand allows you to replace any new activity that is not working well or to conveniently amend an activity in order to suit a class' particular needs. You will find that such a file box will come in very handy when the overhead projector suddenly stops working or when you have extra time left at the end of a class. Such a box may be useful to the substitute teacher if you are lucky enough to have one who knows the language you are teaching.

We would like to encourage you to write to us in care of James J. Asher (Sky Oaks Productions, P.O. Box 1102, Los Gatos, California 95031) and let us know which of these games are *your* favorites, along with tips for variations or for improving the effectiveness of the games in the classroom.

7. Bibliography

Allen, Robert L. "The Use of Rapid Drills in the Teaching of English to Speakers of Other Languages." TESOL Quarterly 6,1 (March 1972): 13-32.
Excellent combination of play with practice. Describes specific activities.

American Council on the Teaching of Foreign Languages (ACTFL). Games for the Foreign Language Classroom. New York: ACTFL Materials Center, n.d. 22 pp.
Detailed descriptions of Spanish and French versions of a marketing game; brief outlines of miscellaneous foreign language games. Mimeographed.

Asher, James J. *Learning Another Language Through Actions (6th Edition)* Sky Oaks Productions, Inc.,
P.O. Box 1102, Los Gatos, CA 95031
(To order online, click on **www.tpr-world.com**)

Asher, James J. *Brainswitching: Learning on the Right Side of the Brain.* Sky Oaks Productions, Inc.,
P.O. Box 1102, Los Gatos, CA 95031
(To order online, click on **www.tpr-world.com**)

Asher, James J. *A Simplified Guide to Statistics for Non-Mathematicians.* Sky Oaks Productions, Inc.,
P.O. Box 1102, Los Gatos, CA 95031
(To order online, click on **www.tpr-world.com**)

Asher, James J. *Brainstorming Kit.* (booklet and transparencies), Sky Oaks Productions, Inc.,
P.O. Box 1102, Los Gatos, CA 95031
(To order online, click on **www.tpr-world.com**)

Asher, James J. *Original Prize-Winning TPR Research Articles* (booklet and CD), Sky Oaks Productions, Inc.,
P.O. Box 1102, Los Gatos, CA 95031
(To order online, click on **www.tpr-world.com**)

Asher, James J. *The Super School: Teaching on the Right Side of the Brain.* Sky Oaks Productions, Inc.,
P.O. Box 1102, Los Gatos, CA 95031
(To order online, click on **www.tpr-world.com**)

Asher, James J. *The Weird and Wonderful World of Mathematical Mysteries: Conversations with famous scientists and mathematicians.* Sky Oaks Productions, Inc.,
P.O. Box 1102, Los Gatos, CA 95031
(To order online, click on **www.tpr-world.com**)

Asher, James J. *Learning Algebra on the Right Side of the Brain.* You can read this article on the web by clicking on
www.tpr-world.com

Barlin, Anne, and Paul Barlin. *The Art of Learning through Movement: A Teachers' Manual of Movement for Students of All Ages.* Los Angeles: Ward Ritchie Press, 1971.
"Appreciation of every subject can be amplified when children use their bodies to experience it." Suggests ways in which physical activity can help open up communication, develop fantasy, release fears and angers, increase self-confidence and self-awareness, and involve the student in learning almost any subject.

Carton-Caprio, Dana. "Learning by Doing: A Practical Foreign Language Experience." *Modern Language Journal* 59, 3 (1975): 97-100.
Describes a shopping game. Students bring "white elephants" to class and divide into groups to choose a store name; label and price objects; get money from the "bank"; and take turns buying and selling objects from each other's stores—all in French.

Chappel, Bernice M. *Listening and Learning: Practical Activities for Developing Listening Skills.* Belmont, California: Fearon Publishers, 1973. 120 pp.
Suggestions for activities and discussion questions. Seventy-six lessons of 5 to 15 minutes each. Many activities and questions are also appropriate for reading comprehension exercises. Intended for primary grades but appropriate for older students.

Criscuolo, Nicholas P. *137 Activities for Reading Enrichment.* Dansville, New York: The Instructor Publications, Inc., 1975. 48 pp.
Activities intended for elementary pupils but appropriate for older students. Organized into 11 categories: word analysis, vocabulary, main ideas, sequence of ideas, comprehension, critical reading, study skills, oral reading, recreational reading, book reports, and bonus activities.

Dorry, Gertrude Nye. *Games for Second Language Learning.* New York: McGraw-Hill, 1977. 56 pp.
Games classified by objective, materials required, and level of advancement. Developed for teaching English as a second language. Half page per game.

Emmons, Marilyn C. "The General Information Quiz as a FL Training Tool." *Accent on ACTFL* (November 1975): 4-5.
Describes a bingo-style quiz in which students cross off terms as the teacher reads their definitions aloud. Designed to show students that "it is possible to comprehend statements in this new idiom even though the actual words may not have been encountered on any vocabulary list."

Galyean, Beverly. *Language from Within.* Santa Barbara, CA: Confluent Education Development and Research Center, 1976. 109 pp.
Specific game descriptions.

Garcia, Ramiro. *Instructor's Notebook: How to Apply TPR for Best Results*. (Triple expanded fourth edition.) Los Gatos, California: Sky Oaks Productions, Inc., 1996.
(See ad page in back of this book for ordering information.)

-------*Instructor's Notebook: Homework Exercises*. (Sequel to Instructor's Notebook.) Los Gatos, California: Sky Oaks Productions, Inc.
(See ad page in back of this book for ordering information.)

-------*Graphics Book*. (Available in English, German, Spanish and French.) Los Gatos, California: Sky Oaks Productions, Inc.
(See ad page in back of this book for ordering information.)

-------*TPR Bingo*. (Available in English, German, Spanish and French.) Los Gatos, California: Sky Oaks Productions, Inc.
(See ad page in back of this book for ordering information.)

Gattegno, Caleb. *The Common Sense of Teaching Foreign Languages*. New York: Educational Solutions, 1976. 223 pp.
Gattegno developed the "silent way" of language learning. Describes specific activities.

Grobe, Edwin P. *175 Activities for Foreign Language Clubs*. Portland, Maine: J. Weston Walch, 1969. 115 pp.
Both secondary and college level. Games alphabetized by title.

-------*300 Word Games for Foreign Language Classes*. Portland, Maine: J. Weston Walch, 1969. 183 pp.
Both secondary and college level. Games alphabetized by title.

Gutzler, Dorothy, and Helen Lim. *110 Reading Comprehension Activities for Primary, Middle, and Upper Levels*. Dansville, New York: The Instructor Publications, Inc., 1975. 48 pp.
Activities organized into five categories: oral and written clues; vocabulary clues; main ideas; recognizing details; and critical reading.

Hildebrand, Janet. *The College Foreign Language Requirement and Developments in Foreign Language Education, 1967-1973: From 'New Key' to a New Direction*. M.A. thesis, University of Texas at Austin, 1974. 206 pp.
Gives background leading to her choice of a new teaching strategy, a "total involvement" method emphasizing interaction with people and objects in a variety of situations created in the classroom.

Hubbard, Harriet. "Music class acquires more personal note." *American-Statesman*, Austin, Texas, n.d. (fall 1975).
News story on elementary students learning music "the way they learned their native language--gradually, by imitation." German composer Carl Orff's technique of teaching music: the child "is taught how to use his whole body as a musical instrument."

Kalivoda, Theodore B. "Multi-Sensory Exercises." In *Dimension: Languages '75* (Proceedings of the Eleventh Southern Conference on Language Teaching), pp. 84-93. Atlanta: Spelman College, 1976.
Physical response activities: the audio-motor unit.

Kohl, Herbert P. *Math, Writing, and Games in the Open Classroom.* New York: Vintage, 1974. 252 pp.
See also Kohl's *The Open Classroom* (New York: Vintage, 1969). Kohl stresses the importance of the teacher's imagination in devising ways to open up a subject for students and ways to activate the students so that they will learn by doing. He points out that games, which are essentially repetitive and are played over and over, can often assume the same functions that drill does in more traditional learning, i.e., to help people practice skills until they are acquired as habits.

Lee, W. R. *Language-Teaching Games and Contests.* London: Oxford University Press, 1965. 167 pp.
"There are many children's games which adults like playing, particularly if they see the language-learning point..... There is little necessary language-learning work which cannot...be profitably converted...into a game." Games for all ages and achievement levels in five general categories: pronunciation, spelling, oral, reading and writing, and "mixed bag," each subdivided by objective. One paragraph to one page per game.

McIntyre, Mary. "How to humanize the intellectual." *American-Statesman*, Austin, Texas, October 5, 1975.
On secondary art education through inducing kinetic response to static visual art, a program developed by New Yorker Philip Yenawine at the Metropolitan Museum and brought by Yenawine to Laguna Gloria Art Museum in Austin, Texas.

Maidment, Robert, and Russell H. Bronstein. *Simulation Games: Design and Implementation*. Columbus, Ohio: Charles E. Merrill Publishing Co., 1973.
History and uses of simulations, principles of designing simulations, a sample game ("Pollution Control"), a list of commercial games, and a bibliography.

Mellenbruch, Julia. *No Doze for Foreign Language Classes*. Austin, Texas: Austin Independent School District, 1975. 16 pp.
Games and simulations to use in the classroom, partially adapted from materials prepared by Beverly Galyean and Barbara Snyder.

Mulac, Margaret E. *Educational Games for Fun*. New York: Harper & Row, 1971. 180 pp.
Describes math, social studies, science, and language games. Designed for elementary, but some seem suitable for secondary. Some games far-fetched and primarily for fun, but some are directly related to learning.

Ogden, Herbert G., Jr. "Team Learning." *Unterrichtspraxis* 7 (1974): 98-99.
Describes team competition games designed to remove the teacher from prominence as a judge and, instead, to encourage student questioning and correcting.

Pate, Glenn S., and Hugh A. Parker, Jr. *Designing Classroom Simulations*. Belmont, California: Lear Siegler, Inc./Fearon Publishers, 1973. 67 pp.
A programmed textbook (branching program or "scrambled format") designed to teach teachers criteria and techniques for effective simulations. Includes some simulation ideas for various fields.

Pearson, Craig, and Joseph Marfuggi. *Creating and Using Learning Games*. Palo Alto, California: Learning Handbooks, 1975. 95 pp.
Focuses on over 50 different types of games, their purposes, and criteria for selecting and creating the most useful games. Suitable for elementary and secondary schools.

Schmidt, Elisabeth. *The German Club in High School.* Skokie, Illinois: National Textbook Company, 1970. 121 pp.
The chapter on games includes suggestions for riddles, tongue twisters, guessing games, games with signs and labels, and charades. Activities suggested for programs and projects are also useful for class enrichment projects.

_____.*Let's Play Games in German.* Skokie, Illinois: National Textbook Company, 1970. 81 pp.
Games classified by main focus: number, category, map, song, etc. Each game description (1/2 to 1 page) includes aim, materials needed, and description in English, with dialogue in German and English.

Shears, Loyda M., and Eli M. Bower, eds. *Games in Education and Development.* Springfield, Illinois: Charles C. Thomas, Publ., 1974.
See especially the article by James H. Humphrey, "Child Learning Through Active Games," which reports that more significant learning takes place when motor activity is linked with verbalized concepts in science, math, and reading and suggests specific activities; and also the article by Perry Gillespie, "A Model for the Design of Academic Games," which is intended for the construction of secondary as well as elementary level games.

Silvers, Stephen M. *The Command Book.* Los Gatos, California: Sky Oaks Productions, Inc., 1988.
How to use TPR with 2,000 high-frequency words used in beginning and intermediate language textbooks.

Smith, Clyde. "German Circle Games: A Motivational Grammar." Manuscript. 1978.
Describes each game in detail. Highly structured games for practicing specific structures and vocabulary.

Stanislawczyk, Irene E., and Symond Yavener. *Creativity in the Language Classroom.* Rowley, Massachusetts: Newbury House Publishers, 1976. 101 pp.
Describes numerous activities designed to encourage creative use of language, classified by beginning, intermediate, and advanced classes, with an additional chapter of activities to teach students about foreign cultures. (Note: Newbury House is now a division of Harper and Row.)

Sullivan, Dorothy D., and James H. Humphrey. *Teaching Reading Through Motor Learning*. Springfield, Illinois: Charles C. Thomas, Publisher, 1973. 149 pp.
Theoretical (educational psychology) background, criteria for game development, and description of specific games.

Wagner, Rudolph F. *Lingua-Games*. Portland, Maine: J. Weston Walch, Publisher, 1958. 36 pp.
Twenty games, described in detail (1-2 pages each), useful for any school or college foreign language classroom (in English; only a few examples in foreign languages). For each game: objectives, materials needed, introduction, game description.

_____. *Successful Devices in Teaching German*. Portland, Maine: J. Weston Walch, Publisher, 1959, rev. 1971. 150 pp.
Collection of learning and teaching activities. Ten chapters, and appendix containing bibliography of sources for teaching materials.

Willes, Burlington. *Games and Ideas for Teaching Spanish*. Belmont, California: Fearon Publishers, Inc., 1967. 33 pp.
Games organized by objective. Descriptions in English but includes some Spanish vocabulary, mainly titles for the games.

Winford, Phyllis. *Teacher-Made Materials: Games and Other Things*. Austin, Texas: Austin Writers Group, 1973. 98 pp.
Guidelines for making simulation and other teaching games for social studies, math, language, and other areas, using poster board, felt pens, etc., with thorough instructions.

Woodruff, Margaret S. *Comprehension-Based Language Lessons: Level I*. Los Gatos, California: Sky Oaks Productions, Inc., 1986. xxx, 232 pp.
Detailed lesson plans for a total physical response introduction to German or English (30 hours), including many games and complete teacher scripts.

TPR PRODUCTS

Books • Games
Student Kits
Teacher Kits
Audio Cassettes
Video Demonstrations

Order directly from the publisher using your
VISA, MASTERCARD, or DISCOVER CARD
WE SHIP ASAP TO ANYWHERE IN THE WORLD!

Sky Oaks Productions, Inc.
P.O. Box 1102
Los Gatos, CA 95031 USA

Phone: (408) 395-7600 • Fax: (408) 395-8440
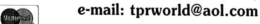e-mail: tprworld@aol.com

FREE CATALOG UPON REQUEST!

To order online, click on:

www.tpr-world.com

Expanded 6th Edition!

Our Best Seller !!

✓ **Demonstrates** step-by-step **how to apply TPR** to help children and adults acquire another language **without stress.**

✓ More than **150 hours** of **classroom-tested TPR lessons** that **can be adapted to teaching any language** including Arabic, Chinese, English, French, German, Hebrew, Japanese, Russian, and Spanish.

✓ A behind-the-scenes look at how **TPR** was developed.

✓ **Answers more than 100 frequently asked questions** about **TPR.**

Learning Another Language Through Actions

by
James J. Asher
Originator of the

Total Physical Response

6th Edition
Over 50,000 Copies in Print!

✓ **Easy to understand** summary of 25 years of research with Dr. Asher's world famous **Total Physical Response.**

NEW FEATURES IN THE 6TH EDITION
• **Frequently Asked Questions - Newly Expanded!**
• **Letters from my mailbag**
• **e-mail addresses for TPR instructors around the world**

Order #201

Order from anywhere in the world with your Visa/Mastercard, check, money order, or official school purchase order.
Sky Oaks Productions, Inc. P.O. Box 1102, Los Gatos, CA 95031 USA • Phone: (408) 395-7600 • Fax: (408) 395-8440

Brainswitching:
Learning on the Right Side of the Brain

2nd Ed. - 308 Pages *For __Fast__, __Stress-Free__ Access to* Order #202
Languages, Mathematics, Science, and much, much more!

The Super School:
Teaching on the Right Side of the Brain
To help most students __learn anything fast__
in academics, sports, or technology! Order #204
Your students won't want to miss a single class!

New! The Weird and Wonderful World of

Mathematical Mysteries
Conversations with famous scientists and mathematicians.
by James J. Asher Order #91a

Exclusive - New discovery __published here for the first time__ solves a 2,000 year old mystery that baffled such famous people as Pythagoras, Euclid, Sir Isaac Newton, and Einstein.

- With TPR, I demonstrate how to remove the fear of learning foreign languages. With this new book, I show you how to __remove the fear of mathematics__.

- My conversations with famous scientists and mathematicians reveals their secret strategy for making spectacular breakthroughs by __playing with ideas on the right side of the brain__.

- I demonstrate how anyone who can do simple arithmetic __has a shot at world fame__ by finding hidden patterns in nature!

New!
A Simplified Guide to Statistics
for Non-Mathematicians: Order #265
How to organize a successful research project.
by James J. Asher

- How to evaluate the effectiveness of your instructional program to get the support you deserve from your organization.
- Here is my promise: If you can do simple arithmetic, you will understand *every concept* in this easy-to-read book!
- Learn the ABC's of any first-class research program.

Added Bonus: Tips for organizing a successful master's thesis or doctoral dissertation!

New! James J. Asher's
Prize-Winning TPR Research

For the first time collected in one place on a CD, the complete prize-winning body of research by James J. Asher. Booklet available with the CD gives Asher's comments on each study with recommendations for future research. Saves you weeks of searching the internet or library.

- Shows step-by-step how Asher planned and successfully completed each research study.
- Includes all of Asher's pioneer studies in second language learning.

Bonus: Also includes Asher's research in industrial psychology—problem solving, creativity, hiring, training, aptitude testing, and designing the world's first automated postal distribution center.

Order #7-CD

New! James J. Asher's
Brainstorming Kit

Transforms <u>ordinary</u> <u>committee</u> <u>meetings</u> into high-powered problem solving sessions!

- Booklet and Transparencies with step-by-step directions to guide your brainstorming group.
- Helps your group understand what to do and why they are doing it.
- Discover options you never thought possible—and it's a lot of fun, too!

Order #8

Best Demonstrations of Classic TPR *Anywhere in the World!*

James J. Asher's Classic Videos demonstrate the original research...

Historic videos show the original TPR research by Dr. James J. Asher with children and adults learning Japanese, Spanish, French and German. We include with every video cassette a copy of the scientific publications documenting the amazing results you will see.

A must for anyone teaching TPR. Each video is unique, and shows different stress-free features of TPR instruction — *no matter what language you are teaching,* including English as a Second Language.

(Each video is narrated in English.)

Children Learning Another Language: *An Innovative Approach*© | Order #435 |

Color, 26 minutes, shows the excitement of children from K through 6th grades as they acquire **Spanish** and **French** with **TPR**. (ESL students will enjoy this too!)

If you are searching for ways that motivate children to learn another language, don't miss this classic video demonstration. The ideas you will see can be applied in your classroom for any grade level and for any language, including English as a second language.

Motivational Strategy for Language Learning© | Order #406 |

Color, 25 minutes, demonstrates step-by-step how to apply **TPR** for best results with students between the ages of 17 and 60 acquiring **Spanish**. Easy to see how **TPR can be used to teach any target language.**

See the excitement on the faces of students as they understand everything the instructor is saying in Spanish. After several weeks in which the students are silent, but responding rapidly to commands in Spanish, students spontaneously begin to talk. You will see the amazing transition from understanding to speaking, reading, and writing!

Strategy for Second Language Learning© | Order #407 |

Color, 19 minutes, shows students from 17 to 60 acquiring **German** with **TPR**. Applies to any language!

Even when the class meets only two nights a week and no homework is required, the retention of spoken German is remarkable. You will be impressed by the graceful transition from understanding to speaking, reading, and writing!

Demonstration of a New Strategy in Language Learning© | Order #408 |

B&W, 15 minutes, shows American children acquiring Japanese with TPR. Applies to any language! This is the first demonstration of the Total Physical Response ever recorded on film when American children rapidly internalize a complex sample of Japanese. You will also see the astonishing retention one year later! Narrated by the Originator of TPR, James J. Asher.

Dear Colleague:

Language instructors often say to me, "I tried the TPR lessons in your book and my students responded with great enthusiasm, but what can the students do **at their seats**?"

Here are effective TPR activities that students can perform **at their seats**. Each student has a kit such as the interior of a kitchen. Then you say in the target language, "Put the man in front of the sink." With your kit displayed so that it is clearly visible to the students, you place the man in the kitchen of your kit and your students follow by performing the same action in their kits.

As items are internalized, you can gradually discontinue the modeling. Eventually, you will utter a direction and the students will quickly respond without being shown what to do.

Each figure in the **TPR Student Kits** will stick to any location on the playboard **without glue**. Just press and the figure is on. It can be peeled off instantly and placed in a different location over and over.

You can create fresh sentences that give students practice in understanding hundreds of useful vocabulary items and grammatical structures. Also, students quickly acquire "function" words such as **up, down, on, off, under, over, next to, in front of,** and **behind**.

To guide you step-by-step I have written ten complete lessons for each kit (giving you about 200 commands for each kit design), and those lessons are now available in your choice of **English, Spanish, French,** or **German**. The kits can be used with **children or adults** who are learning **any language** including **ESL** and the **sign language of the deaf**.

About the TPR Teacher Kits

Use the **transparencies** with an overhead projector to flash a playboard on a large screen. Your students **listen** to you utter a direction in the target language, **watch** you perform the action on the large screen, and then follow by performing the same action in their **TPR Student Kits**.

Best wishes for continued success,

James J. Asher

Back By Popular Demand!
Buy 6 Kits (Student or Teacher) in any assortment
and select an additional kit as our **Free Gift** to you!

James J. Asher's TPR STUDENT KITS™
More than 300,000 Kits now being used in FL-ESL classes throughout the world!!

	ENGLISH Order Number	SPANISH Order Number	FRENCH Order Number	GERMAN Order Number	DUTCH Order Number
Airport ©	4E	4S	4F	4G	4D
Beach ©	12E	12S	12F	12G	12D
Classroom ©	10E	10S	10F	10G	10D
Garden ©	17E	17S	17F	17G	17D
Department Store ©	13E	13S	13F	13G	13D
Farm ©	60E	60S	60F	60G	60D
Gas Station ©	5E	5S	5F	5G	5D
Home ©	1E	1S	1F	1G	1D
Hospital ©	21E	21S	21F	21G	21D
Kitchen ©	2E	2S	2F	2G	2D
Main Street ©	15E	15S	15F	15G	15D
New ➤➤ Office ©	6E	6S	6F	6G	n/a

(Includes high tech business machines: computers, cell phones, fax, and satellite communications!)

	ENGLISH	SPANISH	FRENCH	GERMAN	DUTCH
Picnic ©	16E	16S	16F	16G	16D
Playground ©	20E	20S	20F	20G	20D
Restaurant ©	40E	40S	40F	40G	40D
Supermarket ©	11E	11S	11F	11G	11D
Town ©	3E	3S	3F	3G	3D
United States Map ©	22E	22S	22F	n/a	22D
New ➤➤ European Map ©	23E	23S	23F	23G	23D

(Recently updated to include the Middle East!)

4-KITS-IN-ONE: ©	50E	50S	50F	50G	50D

Calendar © (limited supply) 31   (In English)
TPR Student Kit Stories ©Uses vocabulary from the Student Kits.   **Order Number 33**

James J. Asher's TPR TEACHER KITS™
Transparencies for an **Overhead** **Projector**

*See the TPR Student Kits in **Full Color:** www.tpr-world.com or look in these books:*
* *"Learning Another Language Through Actions"*
* *"Instructor's Notebook: How to apply TPR for best results!"*

	ENGLISH Order Number	SPANISH Order Number	FRENCH Order Number	GERMAN Order Number	DUTCH Order Number
Airport ©	4ET	4ST	4FT	4GT	4DT
Beach ©	12ET	12ST	12FT	12GT	12DT
Classroom ©	10ET	10ST	10FT	10GT	10DT
Garden ©	17ET	17ST	17FT	17GT	17DT
Dept. Store ©	13ET	13ST	13FT	13GT	13DT
Farm ©	60ET	60ST	60FT	60GT	60DT
Home ©	1ET	1ST	1FT	1GT	1DT
Hospital ©	21ET	21ST	21FT	21GT	21DT
Kitchen ©	2ET	2ST	2FT	2GT	2DT
Main Street ©	15ET	15ST	15FT	15GT	15DT
New ➤➤ Office ©	6ET	6ST	6FT	6GT	n/a
Picnic ©	16ET	16ST	16FT	16GT	16DT
Playground ©	20ET	20ST	20FT	20GT	20DT
Supermarket ©	11ET	11ST	11FT	11GT	11DT
New ➤➤ Town ©	3ET	3ST	3FT	3GT	3DT
U.S. Map ©	22ET	22ST	22FT	22GT	22DT
European Map ©	23ET	23ST	23FT	23GT	23DT

For over 25 years, Ramiro Garcia has successfully applied the Total Physical Response in his high school and adult language classes.

This Triple-expanded Fourth Edition (over 300 pages) includes:

✓ Speaking, Reading, and Writing
✓ How to Create Your Own TPR Lessons.

And more than 200 TPR scenarios for beginning and advanced students.

✓ TPR Games for all age groups.
✓ TPR Testing for all skills including oral proficiency.

Instructor's Notebook:
How to Apply TPR For Best Results
By
RAMIRO GARCIA
Recipient of the
OUTSTANDING TEACHER AWARD

Order #225

In this illustrated book, Ramiro shares the tips and tricks that he has discovered in using TPR with hundreds of students. No matter what language you teach, including ESL and the sign language of the deaf, you will enjoy this insightful and humorous book.

New! Just off the press!
THE SEQUEL!!!

Instructor's Notebook:
TPR Homework Exercises
by
RAMIRO GARCIA
Recipient of the
MOST MEMORABLE TEACHER AWARD
and the
OUTSTANDING TEACHER AWARD
Edited by
James J. Asher

Order #224

Ramiro's brand-new companion book to the Instructor's Notebook!

✓ Hundreds of TPR exercises your students can enjoy at home
✓ Catch-up exercises for students who have missed one or more classes.
✓ Review of the classroom TPR experience at home
✓ Helps other members of the student's family to acquire another language.
✓ Helps the teacher acquire the language of the students with exciting self-instructional exercises!

The Graphics Book©

For Students of All Ages acquiring English, Spanish, French, or German

by RAMIRO GARCIA

Dear Colleague;

You recall that I introduced graphics in the Instructor's Notebook. Hundreds of teachers discovered that **students of all ages** thoroughly enjoyed working with the material.

Your students understand a huge chunk of the target language because you used TPR. Now, with my new graphics book, you can follow up with **300 drawings** on tear-out strips that help your students zoom ahead with **more vocabulary, grammar, talking, reading** and **writing** in the target language.

In this book, you will receive **step-by-step guidance** in how to apply the graphics effectively with **children and adults** acquiring <u>any</u> language including **ESL**.

As an **extra bonus**, I provide you with **60 multiple-choice graphic tests for beginning and intermediate students.**

Order **The Graphics Book** directly from the publisher, Sky Oaks Productions in your choice of English (228), Spanish (229), French (236), or German (237).

Order from anywhere in the world with your Visa/Mastercard/DiscoverCard, check, money order, or official school purchase order.

Sky Oaks Productions, Inc. P.O. Box 1102, Los Gatos, CA 95031 USA • Phone: (408) 395-7600 • Fax: (408) 395-8440

TPR BINGO©

by RAMIRO GARCIA

In 25 years of applying the **Total Physical Response** in my high school and adult Spanish classes, **TPR Bingo** is the one game that students ask to play over and over!

When playing the game, students hear the instructor utter directions in the target language.

As they advance in understanding, individual students

Use your Visa. Mastercard, or Discover Card to order from anywhere in the world • We ship ASAP!

ask to play the role of caller, which gives them valuable practice in reading and speaking. For an extra bonus, students internalize numbers in the target language from 1 through 100.

TPR Bingo comes with complete step-by-step directions for playing the game and rules for winning. There are 40 playboards (one side for beginners and the reverse side for advanced students). A master caller's board is included, with 100 pictures, chips, and caller-cards in your choice of **English (226E), Spanish (226S), French (226F),** or **German (226G).**

As I tell my colleagues, "Try this game with your students. You will love it—they will love it!"

Brand-new feature!
Now included in every order of TPR Bingo...
Play TPR Bingo with your students to move them from the imperative to the declarative (and interrogative). It's easy, it's fun, and you will love it!

TPR for Children of All Ages!

For 30 years, "Listen & Perform" worked for children of all ages learning English in the Amazon - and it will work for your students too!

Order this popular Student Book in your choice of **ENGLISH, SPANISH** or **FRENCH**!

Your students will enjoy more than 150 exciting pages of stimulating right brain **Total Physical Response** exercises such as: *drawing* • *pointing* • *touching* *matching* • *moving people, places, and things*

With the **Student Book** and companion **Cassette**, each of your students can perform <u>alone at their desks</u> or <u>at home</u> to advance from comprehension to sophisticated skills of speaking, reading, and writing! These books by **Stephen M. Silvers** are chock-full of fun and productive TPR activities for older students too!

TPR for Young Children!

- Marvelously **simple format:** Glance at a page and instantly move your students in a logical series of actions.
- **Initial screening test** tells you each student's skill.
- After each lesson, there is a **competency test** for individual students.
- Recommended for beginning students in **preschool**, **kindergarden**, and **elementary**.

Order in **English (#240)**, **Spanish (#241)**, or **French (#242)**.

LEARNING WITH MOVEMENTS

by Nancy Márquez

TPR
Total Physical Response

TOTAL PHYSICAL RESPONSE
IN
THE
FIRST YEAR

By
Dr. FRANCISCO L. CABELLO
with **William Denevan**

In your choice of
English (#221), **Spanish (#220)**, or **French (#222)**

Dear Colleague:

I want to share with you the **TPR Lessons** that my high school and college students have **thoroughly enjoyed** and **retained** for weeks—even months later. My book has...

- A step-by-step script with props for each class.
- A command format that students thoroughly enjoy. (Students show their understanding of the spoken language by successfully carrying out the commands given to them by the instructor. **Production** is delayed until students are ready.)
- Grammar taught implicitly through the imperative.
- Tests to evaluate student achievement.

Sincerely,

Francisco Cabello, Ph.D.

How to TPR Vocabulary!

- Giant 300 page resource book, alphabetized for quick look-up.
- Yes, includes abstractions!
- Yes, you will discover how to TPR 2,000 vocabulary items from Level 1 and Level 2 textbooks.

Look up the word... How to TPR it

Where 1. Pedro, stand up and run to the door. Maria, sit **where** Pedro was sitting. 2. Write the name of the country **where** you were born. 3. Touch a student who's from a country **where** the people speak Spanish (French, English).

For all ages! | Order #273 |

The Command Book

How to TPR 2,000 Vocabulary Items in Any Language

by STEPHEN SILVERS

How to TPR Grammar!
For Beginning, Intermediate, and Advanced Students of All Ages!
Available for English (#260), Spanish (#261), and French (#262)!

"TPR is fine for commands, but how can I use it with other grammatical features?"
Eric Schessler shows you how to apply TPR for
stress-free acquisition of 50 grammatical features such as:

Abstract Nouns	Future - to be going to	Past Perfect	Present Perfect
Adjectives	Future - Will	Past tense of **Be**	Simple Past
Adverbs	Have - Present and Past	Possessive Case	Simple Present
Articles	Interrogative Verb forms	and **Of** expressions	Singular/Plural Nouns
Conjunctions	Manipulatives	Possessive Pronouns	Subject Pronouns
Demonstratives	Object Pronouns	Prepositions of Place	Tag Questions
Expletives	Past Continuous	Prepositions of Time	Verbs
		Present Continuous	Wh - Questions

Laura J. Ayala

FAVORITE GAMES
FOR
FL - ESL CLASSES

(For All Levels and All Languages)
by
Laura Ayala & Dr. Margaret Woodruff-Wieding

| Order #291 |

Chapter 1: Introduction

Chapter 2: Getting Started with Games
- How to get students involved
- How the games were selected or invented.

Chapter 3: Game Learning Categories
- Alphabet and Spelling
- Changing Case
- Changing Tense
- Changing Voice
- Describing Actions
- Describing Objects
- Getting Acquainted
- Giving Commands
- Hearing & Pronouncing
- Using Correct Word
- Statements & Questions   Order
- Negating Sentences
- Telling Time
- Numbers and Counting

Chapter 3 (Cont.)
- Parts of the Body and Grooming
- Plurals and Telling How Many
- Possessive Adjectives & Belonging
- Recognizing Related Words

Chapter 4: Games by Technique
- Responding to Commands
- Listing
- Guessing
- Associating
- Simulating
- Sequencing
- Matching
- Categorizing

Chapter 5: Special Materials For Games
- Objects
- Cards
- Stories
- Authentic Props
- Pictures

Chapter 6: Bibliography

Actionlogues

By Jody Klopp

More LIVE ACTION in English, Spanish, French, or German!

✔ 25 happenings come to life in 396 photographs!

Examples: Getting ready for work, making a sandwich, going on a date, driving a car, etc.

✔ Internalize 160 verbs.

✔ Native speaker on a cassette utters each direction in the target language. Listen and understand instantly by looking at a photo.

✔ **Added Bonus:** Great way for non-native language teachers to expand vocabulary.

TPR IS MORE THAN COMMANDS —*AT ALL LEVELS*
CONTEE SEELY & ELIZABETH ROMIJN | Order #95 |

Winner of the EXCELLENCE IN TEACHING AWARD from the California Council for Adult Education

Explodes myths about Total Physical Response:
  Myth 1: TPR is limited to commands.
  Myth 2: TPR is only useful at the beginning.
Shows how to use James Asher's approach—
✔ to overcome problems typically encountered when using TPR,
✔ to teach tenses and verb forms in any language in 6 ways,
✔ to teach grammar, idioms, and fluent discourse in a natural way,
✔ to help your students tell stories that move them into fluent speaking, reading, and writing.

Shows you how to go from zero to correct spoken fluency with TPR. Very practical, with many examples.

Prize-Winning!
COMPREHENSION BASED LANGUAGE LESSONS
by Margaret S. Woodruff, Ph.D.

Here are **detailed lesson plans** for **60 hours** of **TPR Instruction** that make it **easy** for novice instructors to apply the **total physical response** approach **at any level.** The **TPR lessons** include

- Step-by-step directions so that instructors in any foreign language (including ESL) can apply comprehension training successfully.
- Competency tests for the 10th and 30th lessons.
- Dozens of retested short exercises— to capture student interest.
- Many photographs

Winner of the
Paul Pimsleur Award
(With Dr. Janet King Swaffar)
Illustrations and photographs
by Del Wieding

NOTE! We have printed the lessons in English and German, but we have charged you only the cost of printing a single language.

| Order #290 |

Look, I Can Talk!
Original Student Book for Level 1

Step-by-step, Blaine Ray shows you how to tell a story with **physical actions**, then have your students *tell the story to each other* in their own words **using the target language**, then **act** it out, **write** it and **read** it. Each **Student Book for Level 1** comes in your choice of *English, Spanish, French* or *German* and has

- ✔ 12 main stories
- ✔ 24 additional action-packed picture stories
- ✔ Many options for retelling each story
- ✔ Reading and writing exercises galore.

Blaine *personally guarantees* that each of your students will eagerly tell stories in the target language by using the **Student Book.**

Follow the steps in the **Teacher's Guidebook** and work story-by-story with the **Overhead Transparencies.**

Order #	Title:	
110	**Look, I Can Talk!** *Teacher's Guidebook for All Languages* (In English)	
115	**Look, I Can Talk!** *Student Book for Level 1* - **English**	
116	**Look, I Can Talk!** *Student Book for Level 1* - **Spanish**	**This is the original**
117	**Look, I Can Talk!** *Student Book for Level 1* - **French**	**book that started**
118	**Look, I Can Talk!** *Student Book for Level 1* - **German**	**TPRS!**
111	**Look, I Can Talk!** *Overhead Transparencies for All Languages*	

Look, I Can Talk <u>More</u>!

Once again Blaine uses his exciting technique of blending **physical actions** with interesting story lines to get the students **talking, reading,** and **writing** in the **target language**. This second series of stories continues to build vocabulary while focusing on more advanced grammatical concepts common to second year language classes (i.e., use of infinitives, reflexive verbs, direct and indirect object pronouns, preterite vs. imperfect, etc.) Students enjoy using the target language to describe the stories as well as stories they have created.

Order #	Title::
120	**Look, I Can Talk <u>More</u>!** Student Book for Level 2 - **English - Level 2 ESL**
122	**Look, I Can Talk <u>More</u>!** Student Book for Level 2 - **Spanish - Level 2 Spanish**
123	**Look, I Can Talk <u>More</u>!** Student Book for Level 2 - **French - Level 2 French**
121	**Look, I Can Talk <u>More</u>!** Student Book for Level 2 - **German - Level 2 German**
124	**Look, I Can Talk <u>More</u>!** *Overhead Transparencies for All Languages*

Look, I'm <u>Still</u> Talking!

Order #	Title:
125	**Look, I'm <u>Still</u> Talking!** *Student Book for Level 3* - **English - Level 3 ESL**
126	**Look, I'm <u>Still</u> Talking!** *plus Mini-stories* - **Spanish - Level 3 Spanish**
127	**Look, I'm <u>Still</u> Talking!** *Student Book for Level 3* - **French - Level 3 French**
128	**Look, I'm <u>Still</u> Talking!** *Student Book for Level 3* - **German - Level 3 German**
724	**Look, I'm <u>Still</u> Talking!** *Overhead Transparencies for All Languages*

Fluency Thru TPR Storytelling

How to use storytelling for best results at any level. Frequently Asked Questions, and much, much more! | Order #96

TPR Storytelling
especially for students in
elementary and middle school
by
Todd McKay
It works for high school, too!

✔ Pre-tested in the classroom for 8 years to guarantee success for your students.

✔ Easy to follow, step-by-step guidance each day for three school years - one year at a time.

✔ Todd shows you how to switch from activity to activity to keep the novelty alive for your students day after day.

✔ Evidence shows the approach works: Students in storytelling class outperformed students in the traditional ALM class.

✔ Each story comes illustrated with snazzy cartoons that appeal to students of all ages.

✔ There is continuity to the story line because the stories revolve around one family.

✔ Complete with tests to assess comprehension, speaking, reading and writing.

✔ Yes, cultural topics are included.

✔ Yes, stories include most of the content you will find in traditional textbooks including vocabulary and grammar.

✔ Yes, included is a brief refresher of classic TPR, by the originator— Dr. James J. Asher.

✔ Yes, games are included.

✔ Yes, your students will have the long-term retention you expect from TPR instructions.

✔ Yes, Todd includes his e-mail address to answer your questions if you get stuck along the way.

✔ Yes, you can order a video demonstration showing you step-by-step how to apply every feature in the Teacher's Guidebook.

Order Number	Title
400	Student Book - Year 1 **English**
401	Student Book - Year 2 **English**
402	Student Book - Year 3 **English**
410	Student Book - Year 1 **Spanish**
411	Student Book - Year 2 **Spanish**
412	Student Book - Year 3 **Spanish**
420	Student Book - Year 1 **French**
421	Student Book - Year 2 **French**
422	Student Book - Year 3 **French**
430	Complete Testing Packet for **English** Listening, Reading, Speaking, and Writing
431	Complete Testing Packet for **Spanish** Listening, Reading, Speaking, and Writing
432	Complete Testing Packet for **French** Listening, Reading, Speaking, and Writing
440	Teacher's Guidebook for **English**
441	Teacher's Guidebook for **Spanish**
442	Teacher's Guidebook for **French**
450	Transparencies for All Languages - Year 1
451	Transparencies for All Languages - Year 2
452	Transparencies for All Languages - Year 3
460	TPR Storytelling Video - *Demonstrates each step in the Teacher's Guidebook.*

Exciting new products from Todd McKay!

TPR Index Cards
(Easy-to-handle 4x5 cards)

Available in English (470), Spanish (471), French (472), and German (473)

1. Index cards tell you exactly what to say, lesson by lesson.
2. 60 Cards with vocabulary from First Year textbooks.
3. When your students internalize this vocabulary, they're ready for a smooth transition to stories.
4. No need to fumble through a book.
5. No need to make up your own lessons.
6. Quick! Easy to use! Classroom-tested for success!
7. Works for students of all ages, including adults!

A Second Language Classroom That Works!

New!

Simple TPR Strategies that fill your classes with motivated students eager to learn!

by award-winning language instructor,

Joan Christopherson   *Order # 98*

Dear Colleague,

At my high school, we were disappointed that only 30 percent of the students enrolled in either Spanish or French—then student interest faded after one or two years.

We were determined to transform our foreign language offering into an award-winning program, but how to do it? Well, after many years of trial and error, my colleagues and I developed some very simple TPR Strategies that worked beautifully!

For all languages and all ages!

<u>Result:</u> The demand for foreign languages exploded so much that our school added Russian, Italian, German and Japanese. A remarkable turnaround for any school.

Now I would like to share these TPR Strategies with you. They are quick and simple, and easily adapted to any grade level, any language, and any instructor's teaching style.

Sincerely,

Joan

PS: James Asher's TPR always starts with fast-moving comprehension of the target language in chunks rather than word-by-word.

e-mail: on_the_roaders@yahoo.com

Cutting Edge E-Mail Newsletter for FL/ESL Teachers!

For your free monthly copy of the E-Comp! newsletter
write to Laura Zink de Diaz at:
laura@prolinguistica.com

Printed in the United States
203996BV00001B/34-105/A